PARENTING KIDS WITH EMOTIONAL AND BEHAVIORAL ISSUES

HOW TO GUIDE KIDS' EMOTIONS — LOGICALLY
DEVELOPING THEIR MIND, DISCIPLINING THE
BEHAVIORS, LOVING THE CHILD, AND CHANGING
THEIR ATTITUDE FOREVER

RAVEN T. SCOTT

CONTENTS

In the 8 Life-Changing Secrets to Turning Your Bad Kids Good, you'll learn.....

- Understanding the reasoning behind your child's bad behaviors
- Controlling your child's behavior with these simple techniques every parent should know
- Discover how to maintain the good behavior from your children and lead them to a more happy childhood

To recieve your copy, scan the QR code below or follow this link: http://ravent-scott.com/

INTRODUCTION

"A child whose behavior pushes you away is a child who needs connection before anything else." – *Kelly Barlett*

It's every parent's worst nightmare. Your child comes home from school in a huff, throwing their bags against the wall and kicking their shoes off.

"Hi honey, how are you?" you ask. "Is everything okay?"

"I'm fine! Leave me alone!" they yell, stomping off down the hall and slamming their door. Their music turns up full blast. You go into their room, after knocking gently (even though they can't hear you over the music), and find them huddled up under their bedcovers with their eyes shut tight. "Go away!" they shout again. "I don't want to see you and I don't want to talk to anyone for the rest of the day!"

Yikes. You know something is wrong, that much is obvious. But how do you connect with your child and let them know that they are safe with you, without triggering even more of an emotional outburst? No one wants to be pushed and prodded when they're upset.

What if you have a younger child, though? The situation might go something like this. You're serving lunch—you've lovingly prepared what you know is your three-year-old's favorite meal: tuna sandwiches, cut into squares; orange slices, peeled; carrot sticks, served with ranch dressing. Can't beat that!

Except that apparently, this wasn't what your sweet toddler wanted today. "MOM!/DAD! I'm not eating this!"

"Why not? You always love this lunch."

"I didn't want this today! I'll never eat it again and I hate you!" They kick over their chair and storm out of the kitchen. You hear them crying in their room and when you go to see if you can diffuse the situation with a hug and a conversation, they flail in your arms, kicking and screaming.

Whew. It's tiring just to write it and think about it. It probably makes you tired to read it… especially if you've experienced the situation more than once yourself.

Even though these situations are normal throughout any parenting journey, no one wants them to be the norm. But you need to have tools in your belt for what to do when these things come up.

When you think about it, it's pretty crazy that we create and birth children, then are simply "sent off on our own" to figure it out, oftentimes when we haven't dealt with our own struggles from childhood. Then, on top of that, our society is now structured so that our nuclear family lives within four walls, very far away from our parents, grandparents, siblings, and extended family who were meant to show us the way. Then, even though there might be people next door and across the street who are going about the same journey we are, it's considered taboo to talk about our struggles. So, we just put on a brave face and pretend like there's no dirty laundry to be aired. (What a farce!) To top it off, our children spend most of their days away from us, and then we come back together in the afternoons and evenings, both exhausted from work and school, and are meant to lead and guide our children in growing into flourishing adults when it sometimes seems as if we hardly know each other. What?

We are *all* struggling! Why isn't it okay to ask for help? It should be. It is so important to normalize needing support, to make it okay to say, "I don't know what I'm doing because

I've never seen it done." We need each other, and we need to be able to say, "This is really difficult and I can't go it alone."

I have struggled through those difficult years with uncontrollable children, and I want to give you the theories that will help you understand your child's behavior as well as the practical tips and strategies that will help you (and them) get through the seasons of childhood together... and be better for it. Having an emotional toolbox, if you will, means that you are prepared for any situation that comes your way. Practicing these strategies when it's easy will also make it seem less foreign and frightening when times are hard.

I grew up in the inner cities of Chicago caring for my own five siblings as if they were my own children, with parents who were almost always working. Although I rebelled as a teen—breaking curfews to hang out with friends my parents didn't approve of, stealing clothes and accessories that I would hide in my backpack until I got to school, experimenting with drugs and alcohol... all things I wish I hadn't done but that I am glad have given me the perspective they do—I remember what it was like to feel frustration as a growing child. Now that I have my own family—whom I care for on my own after losing my husband to cancer—I want to share the lessons learned with others so that they can find all the joy that is to be had in raising children... because I believe that joy is there in abundance if you have the right tools. Parenting didn't come easily to me—I struggled with my older kids and had to make many mistakes to find my way. Just like as a teenager, I've said and done things that I wish I didn't, but I learned, grew, and took those lessons to heart. Now I look at others' situations with humility, understanding, and the realization that we all have our own path we're walking.

There is never a struggle we go through in life that isn't worked for good. As humans, we use our struggles that we overcome to help others and guide them on paths to development and joy. I know that raising children, learning how to deal with your own trauma and triggers, and helping other families is what I was meant to do. Since I realized this, I have helped countless friends and family members find their own power in choosing to parent with empathy, respect, and intentional relationships. I have seen firsthand children and parents who were stuck in patterns of negativity, uncontrollable behavior, and toxic communication flip the script and begin enjoying each other the way that they were intended to. I've done countless hours of research, not only in books themselves but in parenting classes, courses, counseling sessions, and community engagements where I've learned about the width and breadth of the parenting experience that I couldn't help but put together into a book of knowledge to help others on their way.

If you're in the trenches of raising children (or maybe you're doing the honorable work of a teacher or caregiver, helping others teach and/or raise children) and you sometimes struggle to get through to them, this book is for you. If you sometimes find that the small humans in your care are uncontrollable, or that they seem to exhibit emotions or behaviors that are dysregulated, and you don't know what to do, this book is for you. If you are exhausted (mentally, physically, emotionally, spiritually) because you seem to be in a constant battle of wills with your children... this book is definitely for you.

You'll learn *why* children (of all ages) exhibit "uncontrollable" behavior. You'll take away tools to help your kids learn to make important life decisions on their own and to learn from the consequences of their mistakes.

You'll get an overview of the many types of parenting styles and understand which ones usually produce kids who are responsible, kind, and trustworthy. You'll discover how to have empathy for your children and how to create an emotional connection that lasts.

This will enable you to love them through the good and bad times (because they are both prevalent). You'll also come away with solid strategies for self-care that will help you fill your own cup... because you can't give from an empty one.

Raising and caring for children is the most important work in the world. It should never be brushed off or looked at as the last thing that takes priority in this busy world of ours. We need to turn it back around and give these children, who depend on us for their very lives, the honor and respect that is due to them by taking it upon ourselves to learn how we can care for them in the best way possible. Then, and only then, will they be able to take on that job for future generations. Mother Teresa said, "If you want to bring happiness to the whole world, go home and love your family." Once you have the tools to do this with joy, you'll never look back.

1

THE PSYCHOLOGY OF AN "UNCONTROLLABLE" CHILD

W hen you're solving any type of problem, it's important to understand the root cause. Imagine that you're working on fixing up a house, and the walls are cracking, so you need to patch them up. The patching might work just fine for a few months or even a couple of years, but soon those cracks will start coming back. Why? Because the cracks are just a symptom of the true problem... the foundation is crumbling. To really fix the problem, you have to fix the foundation.

Human struggles are the same way. Emotional dysregulation, temper tantrums, non-cooperation, rebellion, negative communication... those are all symptoms of a bigger, more fundamental issue that is going on within a person. To truly connect and solve the problem, and strengthen the relationship at the same time instead of damaging it, the underlying problem needs to be addressed. This chapter will help you understand these root problems that you might already be seeing in the children you're raising or working with. If you haven't seen these yet, reading this will prepare you in case it does come up in the future.

Here, we will try to help you understand the root causes of behavior and emotional challenges that you might have already experienced while raising, teaching, or caring for children.

DEFINING DISORDERS

Before we get into a discussion of possible "disorders" a child might have, it's important to define what a disorder is. Disorder literally means "out of order." It's a pattern of behavior that is outside the variation of normal child ups and downs. Raising kids is difficult, and raising them when they have patterns of disruptive behavior that are outside of the normal range of childhood tendencies is exhausting, frustrating, consuming, and can even be life-altering if you don't get the help and resources you need. You need to understand whether your child is going through a regular life stage or if it's something more serious. This usually isn't easy.

Let's take the good old "temper tantrum," for example. Temper, like a temperature, or to temper something down, means a level. A temper tantrum is a child's level of emotion getting high and out of control, often seemingly out of nowhere. (However, most emotional outbursts or struggles aren't ever "out of nowhere" to the child, even if it seems like it to us on the outside.) A temper tantrum is a normal occurrence during childhood; children are learning how to regulate their emotions, how to name and identify these feelings, and what causes them. They're learning how to react, respond, and cope with the big feelings that are seemingly too big for their little bodies to handle.

However, although temper tantrums can feel exhausting to deal with as a parent or caregiver, they don't necessarily imply that your little one has a problem with authority or struggles with an attention disorder. Labels and diagnoses are a dime a dozen these days: many professionals and doctors want to be able to put a label on a child so that they can prescribe them medication, and many parents want a diagnosis for their child so they can feel like they have an "answer" to what they're struggling with. But humans are complicated, and all the emotions and symptoms of struggles that we exhibit don't always boil down to one "problem." Labels and diagnoses should be kept at a minimum.

As an adult looking for a solution to your child's seemingly problematic behavior, you should first understand *why* children behave as they do. Challenging behaviors can stem from myriad roots: health conditions, unmet emotional needs, lack of or too much stimulation, or genetic traits that can cause struggles, among many other causes.

The term 'disorder' should be used cautiously for children under five years old, as this is a rapid developmental stage. Children who are struggling with emotional or behavioral dysregulation, tantrums, or communication problems will often level out as they grow. However, educating yourself on signs, symptoms, and possible solutions is a smart way to prepare yourself in case things continue to get harder and you need more resources.

Some common early childhood emotional and behavioral conditions that we will explore include Disruptive Mood Dysregulation Disorder (DMDD), Oppositional Defiant Disorder (ODD), conduct disorder, and Attention Deficit Hyperactivity Disorder (ADHD).

Disruptive Mood Dysregulation Disorder (DMDD)

Disruptive Mood Dysregulation Disorder is signified by extreme irritability, anger, and frequent, intense outbursts of emotion. Children struggling with this disorder are at a level beyond an ordinary "moody child." This disorder shows severe emotional impairment that warrants clinical attention.

Someone with DMDD might be irritable or angry for most of the day, almost every day. They often have trouble functioning in one or more of their common places, such as home, school, or with peers, because of said irritability. Their temper outbursts are severe, causing stress or damage to material things or relationships. Young people struggling with this disorder tend to use services and hospitals at higher rates than normal, endure suspensions and expulsions from school, and are prone to developing other mood disorders, such as attention deficit/hyperactivity disorder or generalized anxiety disorders.

The difference between typical irritability and severe irritability is that the latter is characterized by the inability to tolerate frustration. Every child, every person really, becomes irritable from time to time. We all get frustrated; irritation is a natural reaction to this. Outbursts are out of proportion compared to the problem at hand. Typical irritability comes and goes, and can often be tempered quickly or with ease. Severe frustration that comes with DMDD can happen at the drop of a hat, without signs leading up to it, and for reasons that one might not see as a normal "trigger" for an outburst. They aren't able to be solved or soothed without a great deal of attention, communication, or negotiation. These outbursts occur frequently, at least a few times a week.

Children with this disorder are usually diagnosed between six and 10 years old. They need to have been experiencing symptoms for at least a year to qualify for this disorder. These symptoms often evolve with age. For example, an adolescent struggling with DMDD might have fewer tantrums as they grow, but signs of depression and anxiety begin to take their place instead.

DMDD is fairly new, as far as mood disorders go. It has only been in the *Diagnostic and Statistical Manual of Mental Disorders* (DSM) since 2013. DMDD can be treated with a variety of medications or psychotherapy—often a combination of both, but since there hasn't been a great deal of research done on this disorder, current practices are based on other closely related disorders. "Talk therapy" is showing many benefits, and is usually used before medications are prescribed.

If you feel that your child is experiencing symptoms that might warrant another look, then talk to their doctor and report what you've observed, as well as what you've learned through your own research and anecdotal evidence from others. Your child's healthcare provider can help clarify the situation, put things in perspective, and help you come up with a plan for next steps.

It's also a good idea to get a second opinion from a mental health professional. These types of doctors have experience working with youth who struggle with mental and/or emotional disorders that goes beyond a typical pediatrician's practice. They'll be able to help you determine whether your child is struggling from multiple disorders at once (as mentioned above) and if so, what the appropriate methods for treatment might be.

Oppositional Defiant Disorder (ODD)

Oppositional Defiant Disorder is a type of behavior disorder that is usually diagnosed specifically in children. Young people with ODD are defiant, uncooperative, and hostile toward their parents, peers, teachers, and other authority figures. They often cause more trouble to others than they do to themselves. Symptoms include seemingly constant arguing with the majority of adults in a child's life, frequent "temper tantrums," refusing to follow instructions, always questioning rules, speaking harshly to those in authority, and seeking revenge against those who try and enforce regulations.

Researchers don't know what causes ODD, but there are two main theories. The first is the developmental theory, which states that this disorder begins during the toddler stages of life, between 18 months and four years old. Researchers believe that children developing ODD at this stage struggled to learn independence from a caregiver or other person to whom they were emotionally attached. The learning theory states that negative signs and symptoms of ODD are learned behaviors that come from one's environment. Here, researchers believe that children exhibiting signs of ODD are reflecting negative reinforcement shown to them by authority figures in their lives. Continued use of negative reinforcement just exacerbates ODD behaviors because the child is receiving what they crave: reaction and attention.

This could be put up alongside the "nature vs. nurture" theories of personality—are our behaviors, personality, and traits ones that we come with genetically that cannot be avoided, or do we pick them up from our families and experiences? During toddler and teenage years, even children on the "normal" scale of emotions exhibit behaviors similar to ODD. Almost every child experiments with disobedience, arguing, or going against authority, especially if they aren't in a calm state or are hungry, tired, or otherwise upset. However, in children with ODD, these symptoms are the norm, not the exception.

Diagnosis of this disorder should be sought from a healthcare provider, as they will observe the child, compile situational reports from adults, and look for patterns of behavior with possible causes. Treatment includes family, cognitive-behavioral, and peer-group therapy, as well as medications. The earlier that diagnosis and treatment happens, the easier it will be to prevent this disorder from overtaking your child's life.

Parents can help their children by participating in and speaking about therapy in a positive light, following up on and being consistent with appointments, working in a partnership or team with the healthcare provider(s), and reaching out for support when needed.

Prevention isn't necessarily possible, as researchers don't know what causes this disorder. However, it can be possible to take steps to make ODD unlikely. Children exhibiting tendencies toward aggression and uncooperativeness can benefit from early intervention programs that teach anger management and social skills. Talk therapy and school programs to teach about and prevent bullying can also help children in the middle childhood and teenage years. Programs aimed at parent management are also helpful as they give parents the skills to react appropriately to their child's difficult behavior instead of in a way that is inflammatory or that causes the child to shut down.

Conduct Disorder

Conduct disorder the name for a set of emotional and behavioral problems that usually begin during adolescence or childhood. Children with this disorder have a difficult time following rules and behaving in a socially acceptable manner. There are three types of this disorder, categorized according to the age at which the symptoms first present: childhood, adolescence, and unspecified onset.

It can be mild, moderate, or severe. Symptoms are classified into four categories: aggressive conduct, deceitful behavior, destructive behavior, and violation of rules. Boys are usually more likely to engage in aggressive and/or destructive behavior, while girls tend to engage in deceit and rule breaking.

- **Mild Conduct Disorder** – This usually means that a child exhibits enough of the below behaviors to warrant a diagnosis but not more than that. Problems only cause minor amounts of harm, such as lies, skipping school, or breaking curfew.

- **Moderate Conduct Disorder** – If a child exhibits numerous behavior problems that have a mild to severe impact on themselves or others, they will usually fall into this area. Theft, vandalism, or substance experimentation would fall into this category.
- **Severe Conduct Disorder** – If your child's behavior is above mild or moderate, and their choices cause considerable harm to themselves or others, including sexual assault, weapons use, or breaking into property, they would be classified as severe.

- **Aggressive conduct** – This includes intimidation tactics or bullying, harm to people or animals, forced sexual activity, and/or using or threatening use of weapons.
- **Deceitful behavior** – This includes lies, breaking and entering, theft, and/or forgery.
- Destructive behavior – This includes things such as arson, vandalism, slashing tires, or things of the like.
- **Violation of rules** – This includes things like truancy, running away, substance abuse, and very young experimentation with sexual behavior.

There are theories for environmental and genetic causes of conduct disorder. Environmental factors include an abusive childhood, severe family dysfunction, prevalent substance abuse in the home, and extreme poverty. Some research links damage to the frontal lobe (the part of your brain that deals with problem-solving, memory, emotions, and personality) with conduct disorder, causing struggles with impulses, inability to plan and think about future consequences, and an inability to learn from past mistakes.

Children who live in an urban environment, grow up in poverty, who have a family history of mental illness or conduct disorder, and/or who were abused or have a history of chronic trauma are all at higher risk for conduct disorder. Males are also more likely to develop this than females. Diagnosis and treatments are best handled by a mental health professional with the parents' input and support as a united team wanting an improved situation for the child. Children must have at least three behaviors which they exhibit in a continued pattern within the past six months. The behaviors must also impair their functioning at school or in social settings.

Since conduct disorder is so highly influenced by environment, children struggling with this disorder will often be placed into another home. If there is no abuse present in their main home, however, and the parents can provide for the child appropriately, then talk or behavioral therapy will be used to help the child learn to appropriately express their emotions and/or anger. The team of professionals working with the child should also work with the parents, teaching them how to respond to their child and manage their own behavior. Long-term treatment is the norm, but catching this disorder early helps to make the prognosis more positive.

Attention Deficit Hyperactivity Disorder (ADHD)

Attention Deficit Hyperactivity Disorder (ADHD) is often confused with or mislabeled "ADD," but Attention Deficit Disorder is a different diagnosis. ADHD most often starts in children and may continue into adulthood (usually presenting before the age of 12, sometimes as early as three years old). It includes a combination of persistent problems such as difficulty sustaining attention, impulsive behavior, and hyperactivity. Children with ADHD may struggle with low self-esteem, poor performance in school, and troubled relationships.

This disorder is characterized by inattention (wandering off of tasks, lack of persistence), hyperactivity (moving about constantly, even when it is inappropriate or unnecessary for the specific task at hand), and impulsivity (making hasty decisions at the moment without thinking about the potential harm). Children with ADHD are usually placed into one of three subtypes: mostly inattentive, mostly hyperactive or impulsive, or a combination.

Symptoms of inattention can fall within the following:

- Failing to pay attention to details or making careless mistakes
- Trouble staying focused, both in academics and in play
- Not listening, even when addressed directly
- Struggle to complete tasks, schoolwork, or chores
- Difficulty organizing required activities
- General dislike or avoidance of activities that require mental effort
- Frequent loss of materials, toys, or school items
- Ease of distraction
- Forgetfulness of routine daily activities

Symptoms of hyperactivity and/or impulsivity can fall within the following:

- Frequent fidgeting or squirming
- Trouble staying seated or still
- Being in "constant motion"
- Climbing, running, or moving around when inappropriate
- Struggling to play or engage in quiet activities
- Seemingly constant talking
- Interrupting
- Trouble waiting their turn

- Intruding on others' space, activities, or conversations

Remember, as with other disorders, it is normal for children to exhibit behaviors like these here and there or in certain types of situations (e.g., when overstimulated, tired, hungry, frustrated, or cooped up). However, once these become a consistent pattern and start to negatively affect the child's home, school, and social life, then it is probably time to seek professional help.

Risk factors for ADHD include genetics, low birth weight, brain injuries, exposure to environmental toxins, and maternal drug use while pregnant. ADHD is more common in males than in females and is more common if other family members have it as well. Diagnosis requires a comprehensive examination by a licensed clinician such as a psychiatrist, psychologist, or pediatrician. Treatment options include medication and psychotherapy.

An ADHD diagnosis doesn't directly cause other disorders. However, children who struggle with ADHD are more likely to also develop conduct disorder, ODD, general mood and/or anxiety disorders, substance abuse, learning disabilities, tics, disruptive mood dysregulation disorder, and/or to be placed on the autism spectrum.

TIPS FOR PARENTS WHEN DEALING WITH A DISORDER OR DIAGNOSES

If you and your family are struggling with the symptoms that show potential for a mood disorder diagnosis, or have been diagnosed and don't know where to turn next, there are many ways you can help get your bearings about you.

- **Do your own research** – There is so much information out there. Look for news articles about the disorders, search out videos from reputable sources, and read books that they recommend. Stay up on clinical trials. Talk to professionals and ask questions about risks, benefits, and treatments. You have options, so don't take anything at face value if it doesn't sit well with your gut.

- **Talk to the professionals who know your child** – There's nothing more valuable than the experiences of your child's own teachers, counselors, or school psychologists. Not only are they experienced in their field, but they can apply that knowledge to your child specifically. They can also help you come up with plans in the interim until long-term goals are decided upon.

- **Manage your own stress** – If you aren't in a calm, peaceful state of mind, you won't be able to help your child get there either. Having a child with a mood disorder is stressful, but you can implement self-care strategies to help make sure you're handling it all to the best of your ability.

- **Seek support and help for yourself, too** – Your child isn't the only one struggling. It's important for you to have support groups, your own counselor or therapist, and people who you can speak to about everything you're feeling and dealing with.

- **Enable open communication across all lines** – Every resource and support person you have, including health care providers, is part of an intricate team. Keep the professionals up to date with plans and goals, and involve your child in the discussion and options for treatment. When everyone can work together more closely, it will help ensure success.

SCENARIOS FOR CONCRETE UNDERSTANDING

Sometimes it can be helpful to understand a situation if you can "hear" or "see" it happening. Each chapter in this book will give scripted scenarios of common problems to help you process what you're learning and help you apply it to your life. All names and identifying details are changed.

Disruptive Mood Dysregulation Disorder

Scenario 1: Shawna is a ten-year-old girl displaying patterns of anger and aggression in conjunction with ADHD and a generalized anxiety disorder. She exhibits three to four outbursts of anger on average each week and about two to three weekly incidences of aggression toward others. She also harbors irritable feelings which last for hours or days without respite. Shawna's caregivers and her healthcare professional team decided that about a dozen cognitive-behavioral therapy sessions over a three-month period would be a good place to start. Once these sessions were completed and evaluations were completed, Shawna's anger and aggression incidences appeared much less frequently.

Scenario 2: Jack, an eight-year-old boy, seems to be constantly irritated. Each week he has at least three "temper tantrums"—this has been happening for years. During these temper tantrums, Jack hits, punches, and kicks anyone or anything in his vicinity. At school, he yells at both his peers and his teachers. Jack's parents are worried that he not only won't have any friends, but that eventually he will be expelled. The school therapist refers them to a professional psychologist who gives a diagnosis of DMDD and suggests both parent-training classes as well as cognitive behavioral therapy. Over the last six months, Jack and his parents have begun communicating with each other more effectively, there are positive reports of progress from school, Jack is able to verbalize his emotions more, and the parents are able to minimize their own aggressive responses toward Jack's (less frequent) outbursts.

Oppositional Defiant Disorder

Scenario 1: Raheed is an intelligent boy and a high-achieving student who scores well on tests and seems to have quite high capabilities, but he is often said to do things only when he wants to do them. He has been complaining that he is bullied in school since the third grade—he is now in seventh. Raheed often destroys his classwork and accuses others of ruining it, repeating the accusations over and over. This type of behavior is often exhibited on the playground and at home with his siblings as well—everything is someone else's fault, even when that is obviously not true. However, at home there is a culture of yelling, a strict domineering father, and many punishments for even the slightest offenses. Raheed's therapist connected with him over the subjects that really interested him in school, bonding over commonalities. Game play and artistic journaling helped encourage some breakthroughs that eventually led to a conversation in which Raheed recognized himself in some ODD literature in the therapist's office and agreed that he wanted to live without the conflict in his life.

Scenario 2: During Alana's birth, there was a forceps delivery which caused a possible birth injury that the parents did not know could have been identified until they began struggling. As a baby, Alana seemed to never sleep and would cry uncontrollably. Although Alana hit all her developmental milestones, she began to exhibit behavior in preschool that caused her to be asked to leave more than once. Although she took well to independent activities such as teeth-brushing and getting dressed, she would often refuse to do simple tasks if not asked in "the right way," according to her parents. When she exhibited oppositional behavior, she also seemed to have hyperactive episodes. She became openly hostile and uncooperative, as well as easily annoyed by those close to her. Frustrations at home and at school were always blamed on other people, and she would refuse to take responsibility for any situation. Alana's team decided that occupational therapy, an IEP in school, and allowing for "time away" in a safe, low-sensory space would be provided. Her team also agreed that positive reinforcement would be used both at home and in school. Alana began slowly showing progress that continued as long as the therapies and accommodations stayed in place.

Conduct Disorder

Scenario 1: Frank, a 15-year-old male, has begun engaging in harmful activities over the last two years such as arson to trash cans, self-harm in the way of pulling out his own hair in clumps, impulsive behaviors such as running into the street and dodging cars, and severe aggression often taken out on the family pets. School psychologists referred him out for further assessment and a psychiatrist and his parents agreed to begin "mode deactivation therapy" (MDT), since previous tries with "dialectical behavior therapy" (DBT) did not prove successful. After MDT therapy, he showed less presentation of necessary restrains, physical aggression, and sexual aggression, whereas after DBT all of these were on the rise.

Scenario 2: Bonita, a 10-year-old girl, has been struggling in school for the last four years. She gets sent home often for fighting and bullying, and has been expelled from the last three schools for using intentional weapons such as broken bottles and books to hit her peers. Her neighbors even found three of their pet cats shaved down with her initials carved into their skin. She has even threatened to kill her parents, with drawings showing detailed scenarios. A social worker assigned to her case observed family members at home who abused multiple substances, were in and out of jail, and admitted to possibly neglecting and/or abusing children in emotional and verbal ways. Her therapists worry that they are losing any motivation or positive influence without intensive psychiatric treatment and removal from a potentially abusive home.

Attention Deficit Hyperactivity Disorder

Scenario 1: Stuart, a six-year-old boy whose parents have brought him in for diagnosis, is exhibiting struggles at school and at home. His teachers say that he does not sit in his desk for more than five minutes at a time, often touching and prodding other students or their work. He interrupts the teachers and seems to struggle remembering regular classroom routines. At home, he only wants to watch television and play on the computer, but when he comes away from the screen he seems to be even more agitated than before. Stuart loves to read, however, and can even independently consume third-grade novels with accurate comprehension. His team decides on CBT and play therapy, in which he practices routines and home/school scenarios. His parents agree to use visual charts and positive reinforcement, and Stuart is also given an exercise ball to sit on as well as "fidget toys" when he needs to be at his desk.

Scenario 2: Colette, a nine-year-old girl in fourth grade, has struggled with academics since first grade. Tests showed high academic ability but Colette is always complaining that the classroom is "too distracting." She wasn't often bouncing off the walls, but did seem to chew her hair, nails, and shred things at her desk more often than not. Tammy's parents had read many self-help books, hoping to address her tendencies to talk back and break rules, even though grounding and restriction never seemed to have any effect. Colette expressed frustration and a desire to succeed in school as well as at home, but said that she "was always trying but just couldn't be better." Treatment was deemed best as counseling in conjunction with a low-grade stimulant medication that would be at its peak during school hours.

2

EMPOWERING YOUR CHILD: TOOLS FOR DEALING WITH UNCONTROLLABLE STRESSORS

From a grown person's perspective, childhood might seem like a carefree time–full of playing, imagination, the ability to go throughout your day without worrying about a job, bills, and the constant demands of "adulting." However, children still experience stress in all areas of their lives. Things such as school and academic demands, social dynamics and peer pressure, and the lack of control over their daily lives can take quite a toll on a small human's developing mind, heart, and emotions—especially if there are not enough adults in their lives who are willing to listen and help them process through these hard situations.

This chapter will help provide you with important tools to help you help your children deal with negative challenges.

Parents and caregivers cannot protect children from stress, disappointment, or failure. However, they can help them develop healthy ways of coping and solving everyday problems. In fact, it can be freeing to look at things from this perspective even from infancy: it doesn't have to be our "job" to stop our babies from crying. Babies cry. Children struggle. Life is hard. It is our job, however, to "hold" our children through it—sometimes physically, sometimes mentally, sometimes emotionally.

There are plenty of types of stress in this world, and many of these can be "positive stressors" as they relate to the way they work with our brain and hormones. Positive stress can be the anticipation of a sports game, the unknown of learning a new skill, or the newness of changing schools and making new friends. When these types of events are talked about, prepared for, and processed (usually with positive outcomes), our brains and bodies see them as challenges that we have overcome and learn to anticipate that stress with an "I did it before, I can do it again," type of attitude.

However, oftentimes children are subject to more adult types of stressors that they not only don't have control over, but that they can't understand on their own. Stressful events can have effects on a child's well-being, especially when they are not processed or handled in a beneficial way. When children face uncontrollable stressors such as their parents' divorce, excessive pressure in school, moving often during tumultuous times, or feeling as if they don't have friends, their emotional and behavioral actions might be affected. Since major stressors in children are often chronic, some children might experience high distress levels for prolonged periods.

ACEs, or adverse childhood experiences, are a particular type of traumatic stress that can have an effect on a child's development. Basically, the more ACEs one encounters in their developmental years, the more prone they are to emotional and physical disorders and struggles. ACEs can include things such as abuse, neglect, or violence, witnessing abuse or violence against a loved one, or losing a family member to a negative or unexpected death. They could also include situations such as growing up in a home where the adults abuse substances, struggle with mental health problems, or where parental care is unstable due to prison, jail, or custody disputes. The more ACEs a child "tallies up," the more likely they are to have chronic physical, mental health, and substance abuse disorders. High levels of ACEs are also linked to lowered academic performance, fewer or less profitable job opportunities, and less earning potential.

Society itself, and parents and caregivers, can strengthen their own families or those whom they work with in many ways. To strengthen economic support, it's important to have a household with financial security and to have a job with family-friendly policies. Parents should take part in public education campaigns against violence and adversity, and teach men and boys to be allies against violence. Children who are given the benefits of high-quality childcare and enriching education often get off to a better start, and are more likely to succeed if they are taught skills in social-emotional learning, safe dating and relationship practices, and if the parents approach family life with positive skills. Children and youth can be connected to mentoring and/or after-school programs when parents are not available. It's also important to normalize ACEs as something we all experience, and to be able to reach out to our communities to receive the services of individualized primary medical care, victim-centered services, treatments, and family therapy.

While you are exploring this area of childhood stress, adverse childhood experiences, and community resources to strengthen families, you can empower your children at home or in the caregiving situation by teaching them these three strategies: positive imagery and distraction, developing reasonable proximal goals, and reconstruing situations.

Positive Imagery and Distraction

Using positive imagery and distraction can be a tool for coping with anxious situations, frustration, and fear. Children (and adults!) who struggle with these emotions can handle these upheaving situations with more control when they can visualize themselves in a positive place, manifest themselves into a comfortable situation, and distract themselves with other pleasing thoughts when they cannot remove themselves from a place (physical or otherwise) in which they don't want to be.

This is an important tool for children who are undergoing medical procedures, waiting for a big event in life such as a move or a sibling to be born, or who have constant upheavals in life such as moving back and forth between homes when parents are going through a tumultuous separation. Research shows that children who are taught to use this skill are less anxious in unknown situations, report less pain with medical procedures, and often comply more easily when they are required to do something that they don't enjoy. It also helps them to increase patience when waiting for a reward or a desired activity to take place.

Research shows that children who use benign cognitive and behavioral distractors as a way of managing negative emotions are less prone to behavioral disorders. It also shows that the older a child is, the better able they are to use this skill. Learning this skill as a child can also help once they become adults, as it never does well to dwell on the negative and get "stuck" in a pessimistic mindset.

This skill can be used negatively, however, when it is used in inappropriate situations or when it becomes a way to completely deny frustrating circumstances or stressors. For example, a child who is struggling in school but allows herself to daydream the day away rather than focus on the tasks at hand will not be benefitting from distraction.

Developing Reasonable Proximal Goals

Children usually want to reverse irreversible situations, such as the loss of a parent or pet. For example, children from divorced families will often want their parents to get back together, and the emotional energy put toward wishing and hoping (and sometimes working toward this goal) ends up hurting the child more than dealing with the actual situation.

Sometimes, children strive to be the best at a hobby, sport, or school subject. Children need to persist in their dreams—many accomplished adults were told that they could not make it as children. There is always room for everyone to succeed at something, even if they are not "the cream of the crop," and it's also important for children (again, and adults!) to realize that there are many ways to be good at something. However, some children set and hold unreasonable goals for themselves (sometimes influenced by the adults in their lives), which usually involves being better than other kids at something.

While goals are important motivators, parents and care-givers should help children set realistic goals and plans for achieving them. They can also help children set up plans for reaching these goals and come up with coping mechanisms for what might happen if there are hurdles or obstacles in getting to where they want to go.

Let's say that a child takes up baseball around 12 years old, and joins a league in which most kids on the team have been playing since T-ball. They simply aren't going to have as many skills and as much strength on the field as the others who have been playing for six consecutive years. A goal to "hit more than anyone on the team" is unreasonable at the beginning and could be frustrating if there aren't appropriate smaller goals and timelines to work on. However, if the parents and coaches can set smaller goals (i.e., making contact with the ball at least once a game, moving on every pitch, etc.) and ways to get there (i.e., practicing with a backyard hitting net, playing catch three times a week outside of practice) then they can see that it's more beneficial to be working with *themselves* as a benchmark as opposed to comparing themselves to others.

Sometimes, children have to understand that the goals they have are not necessarily a struggle to attain, but impossible. They have to be guided into letting go of those hopes and dreams so that they can focus on more realistic expectations. For example, a child whose beloved grandparent has died and is wishing every night that they could come back to life is not going to do well to put emotional energy toward this wish. However, once they realize and accept that no one can ever come back from dying, they can focus on special ways to remember their grandparent instead.

Research shows that people who are learning something new usually think about the new skill in one of two ways. They either want to show their intelligence or talent (entity theory) or they want to simply learn a new activity (incremental theory). Those who view new activities from the entity theory view them as a way to show how smart, strong, or capable they are, and when it is a struggle or they fail, they see it as a reflection on themselves. Those who view new opportunities from the incremental theory, however, see intelligence, strength, and talent as skills in and of themselves to be developed over time. They see learning more as a journey as opposed to a destination.

Reconstruing Situations

The way children interpret situations in their lives can play an important role in their emotional reactions to those events. Parents can help children overcome feelings of distress and failure by helping them face the future with a positive attitude. Reconstruing a situation can be a positive way of coping with uncontrollable stress because it shifts a child's perspective from a pessimistic, self-defeating attitude to a more optimistic perspective. Reconstruing involves taking a situation that many would categorize as negative, and "flipping the script" so that it is empowering to that person's growth and development. It doesn't mean brushing things under the rug or ignoring struggles, but rather, processing them in a way to take charge of the situation and use uncontrollable circumstances to one's benefit.

When children, or people in general, construe events or qualities about themselves in a pessimistic, blaming, or derogatory way, they are more prone to passive behavior, withdrawal, and depression compared to those who choose to look at things from an optimistic and efficacious perspective. Children who tend to blame others and look for the negative in a situation, for example, thinking that others are always bullying or out to get them, are more likely to engage in aggressive behavior, as well.

Cognitive therapy has been shown to be beneficial for children struggling to construe situations in a positive light. During these sessions, children are encouraged to identify negative thoughts and to challenge them with an opposing, positive viewpoint. The older a child is, the more help they seem to get from cognitive therapy focused on reconstrual, probably because they have greater metacognitive skills. Metacognition means "thinking about thinking"—the greater one's metacognitive skills, the more they are able to process situations in depth and see many sides of a situation.

One should be careful not to use reconstrual in a way that is maladaptive or taken to an extreme. For instance, a child who gets into fights with others regularly and reconstrues the conflict as everyone else's fault because they don't like them would not be beneficial. Some others who are experiencing heightened forms of chronic trauma might create imaginary personas or reconstrue their lives into "other worlds." Although they might be self-preserving, it could be a dysfunctional coping mechanism.

SKILLS THAT MIGHT BE LACKING

Whatever the trigger, professionals believe that a child struggling with any of these disorders discussed in Chapter 1 might be lacking important skills to help them handle the situation better. Some of these skills might include: impulse control, problem-solving, delaying gratification, negotiating, communicating wishes and needs to adults or peers, knowing what is appropriate or expected in a given situation ("reading the room"), and self-soothing.

Self-regulation is an important skill that should begin to be taught early in life. As humans, we cannot avoid difficult, negative, or unfortunate situations. The goal should, instead, be to learn how to navigate through them. For example, children can be taught to take an overwhelming task, such as cleaning a very messy room, into smaller, more manageable tasks. First, they could pick up the large things taking up a great deal of space, such as pillows, books, then dirty clothes. Then, they could put toys into piles: blocks, game pieces, and stuffed animals. If a child is struggling with a physical task, instead of just expecting them to do the entire thing well on their own from the beginning, they could be taught and guided with the focus on one part first. Take brushing teeth: they could practice putting toothpaste on the brush and then the rest could be taken care of by the parent until the toothpaste skill is mastered. Then they could move on to brushing with their own hand.

When children act out when they are overwhelmed, frustrated, or in an unknown situation, the parent or caregiver can physically and emotionally get "down to their level" and encourage them to breathe, slow down, and reflect. (The physical part is important: when we kneel, sit, or crouch down and look at a child in their eyes, we are less overwhelming to them and can be seen more as a partner as opposed to a towering authority figure.) What is going wrong? What is hard? How can they be in charge of fixing the situation? Help them to name emotions and come up with a plan. Put some of the control back into their court and involved them in the process for growth.

Encourage mindful behavior. Mindfulness helps people to focus on the present, instead of brooding about the past or worrying about the future. Parents should practice this for themselves as well, so that they can be present in the situation with their child and see it as part of the journey, as well.

SCENARIOS FOR CONCRETE UNDERSTANDING

Here are some examples of children using these skills for beneficial emotional growth.

Positive Imagery and Distraction

Scenario 1: Shayne has not regularly seen a dentist over his eleven years of life, since as a young child he had a negative experience and has since expressed a phobia surrounding teeth and dental work. He has a cavity causing him extreme pain, however, and it needs to be filled. His parents involve him in the choice of a pediatric dentist, looking at pictures of the office and discussing what will be involved in the treatment. When they get to the office on the day of the filling, Shayne sits down in a chair that has a mural of outer space painted on the above ceiling. Shayne uses the distraction techniques he has practiced at home to "zone in" on the stars and planets, and visualizes himself as the captain of a spaceship exploring new galaxies. Soon enough, the dentist is "bringing him back to Earth," and Shayne is pleasantly surprised at how painless the procedure actually was.

Scenario 2: Francis' family has recently moved into a new neighborhood in a less affluent part of town, and into a much smaller apartment than their old home. Her parents both lost their jobs during the recession and life is quite different now than it used to be. In the beginning, she was sullen and resentful, constantly "wishing she could just go home." Each night, when her mother or father was tucking her in to sleep, they would imagine beautiful, sprawling landscapes and visualize beautiful places in nature that they wished they could visit. At first, Francis did not participate on her own but her parents kept modeling the practice for her and eventually she would jump in with her own ideas. Francis began drawing pictures of these places to hang on her walls, and would bring in flowers, nut and rock collections, and other pieces of nature to adorn their home. She learned to create a space in which she wanted to be.

Developing Reasonable Proximal Goals

Scenario 1: Chase's family has recently been going through a divorce. Chase, a seven-year-old boy, is quite upset and often tells each parent that the other wants to get back together and "be a family again." Chase's mother acknowledges his feelings of upset and frustration, but doesn't know what else to say. Finally, the parents sat him down together and explained, without vilifying each other, why it was healthier for the parents to live apart and that they both still loved Chase just the same. They suggested that Chase could come up with ideas to make his time with each parent as positive and enjoyable as possible. They made a list of the benefits to having parents that lived in two places, and although the negative emotions were allowed time in conversation and were continued to be addressed, the family tried not to make them the focus.

Scenario 2: Maddison was a teenager when she decided that she wanted to take up ballet. Although she had never danced before, seeing a community production of *The Nutcracker* inspired her to take up the hobby. At first, she was overwhelmed in watching the girls her age rise up onto their pointe shoes and pirouette across the stage, and she also felt "babyish" taking the initial introductory ballet courses with the younger kids. With the encouragement of her instructors and her parents, she decided to look up videos on strengthening the necessary ballerina muscles, practiced on her own each day, and sought out classes for "older beginners."

Maddddison's instructor spoke frankly with her about the fact that her first few recitals would have "supporting roles," but they made a realistic timeline for dance goals and checked them off one by one.

Reconstrual

Scenario 1: Georgia has never been able to walk, due to a birth defect affecting her neurological and physical capabilities. In her early school years, she was angry about her situation and ashamed of the fact that she needed a wheelchair. She would often express that she wished she could "do what the other kids did." However, in middle-elementary school Georgia had a teacher who saw an opportunity for empathy-building and reconstrual. Her teacher encouraged her speak to her classmates about the experience of being in a wheelchair. Although she was initially nervous, Georgia began opening up when her peers expressed curiosity and interest in her "special chair." They began sharing ideas about how Georgia could participate in games and activities, and wanted to help push her around the grounds. From then on, Georgia began to see her situation as a way to gain individual attention in a positive way and as a conversation starter with new friends. She was more involved in peer activities and began to enjoy school much more.

Scenario 2: In an unfortunate riding accident, Jamel fell off of his horse and broke his dominant arm in multiple places. He needed two surgeries and was going to be in a cast for months. Horseback riding had been his "life," and he was devastated. Jamel seemed depressed after the accident, not wanting to participate in any other type of entertainment or activity. His occupational therapists began encouraging other types of ways to be involved with horses, such as going to the stables and feeding, grooming, and simply spending time with the animals, while strengthening his arms and fingers at the same time to prepare for the time when he could get back on a horse. His parents encouraged him to journal about his experiences and draw pictures about what he would do once he could get back to riding. Jamel had never been an avid reader or writer, or as interested in the other aspects of horsemanship, but after the accident he had many other ways to incorporate equine love into his life.

3

PARENTING FOR CHILDHOOD SUCCESS

One's parenting style can affect everything having to do with a child's temperament and approach to the world, from their self-concept (how they feel about themselves) to their physical health. Parents should adopt a healthy parenting style to support healthy growth and development (physical, emotional, mental, and spiritual) because how you interact with your child and discipline them leaves a permanent influence.

This chapter will help you manage the discipline of a child depending on the parenting style to which you subscribe. There are definitely parenting styles that create negative emotions and self-concepts in children. However, there are also myriad styles that help nurture positive self-concept and independent, confident, emotionally intelligent children. There are, though, four main "types" that researchers have identified, each with different characteristics. There are different styles within each type, but the ones that will mainly be explored here are: authoritarian, authoritative, permissive, and uninvolved.

Authoritarian – Does Tough Love Work?

This parenting style is about being stern and strict. It focuses on unquestioning obedience and enforces good behavior through threats, shaming, and other punishments. It is often associated with lower levels of parental warmth and responsiveness as opposed to affection and positive attention.

When a child misbehaves, it might be tempting to enforce good behavior through harsh punishments, threats, and other kinds of psychological control, but research suggests that these tactics don't result in long-term behavioral improvements. Consider what psychologists refer to as "externalizing behavior problems" as symptoms of children with authoritarian parents. Oftentimes these children are disruptive, aggressive, defiant, or exhibit anti-social conduct. Research monitoring child development shows that authoritarian parenting styles lead to more of these challenges.

When behavior of children with authoritarian parents was tracked over many years, it was found that tactics such as threats, harsh punishments, and lack of communication about rationale and reasoning actually resulted in behavior that worsened over time. This doesn't negate the fact that genetics could also be a factor in some of these behavioral problems—there might be a link between children who already show these tendencies, which triggers authoritarian responses from adults who don't know what else to do. Oftentimes, if a parent or caregiver is frustrated, stressed, or feels up against a wall, they will fall back on what they know. It's a classic case of "the chicken or the egg": does misbehavior cause authoritarian responses or do authoritarian parenting choices cause misbehavior? It seems to be both.

Research also shows that children with authoritarian parents are much more likely to engage in substance abuse as they get older: the "fear" of what will happen at home doesn't prevent the experimentation; rather, children and adolescents from authoritarian homes often don't have the social and emotional skills to stand up for themselves or are looking to be a part of a group where they will feel loved and included.

Kids from authoritarian families are less socially adept, less resourceful, and likelier to become involved in bullying behavior. Research from all over the world finds similar conclusions. In the United States, studies found that teenagers from authoritarian homes didn't feel socially accepted by others their age. They were also less independent. When looking at college students, they were more likely to bully other young adults. Chinese researchers found that children raised with this strict and harsh discipline were not as socially competent as others, and had a harder time fitting in. They also found that these children functioned poorly in social situations. Studies from Cyprus linked authoritarianism with bullying as well, on both sides of the spectrum (from perpetrators to victims).

In Turkey, research showed that children raised in authoritarian homes were not as resourceful as those raised with more choice and flexibility. South American research also showed these children to be less socially competent than their peers, which might carry over into adulthood. In Spain, there were more links between this parenting style and bullying, even throughout high school. Researchers from the Netherlands found children subjected to the authoritarian ways were not as helpful or popular as others, and less mature when dealing with moral situations.

The irony with regard to children being less morally mature or capable is that authoritarian parents often see themselves as morality "heroes." However, these parents don't often practice what they preach, which can mean that the children begin to ignore them as they get older. They don't see their parents as valid authority figures to live up to, and often engage in delinquent acts to rebel against the ways that were forced on them. Young adolescents from authoritarian homes also don't feel that they can go to their parents to discuss pressing issues, which leaves them to flounder and become more susceptible to peer pressure in any given situation.

Some research also suggests that authoritarian parenting might lead to more cases of depression, low self-esteem, and anxiety. Brazil, Portugal, and Spain all found that young people from these types of homes have lower levels of self-esteem, and that even after becoming adults, this has an effect on people's levels of life satisfaction or happiness. German researchers linked authoritarianism with anxiety, and American and Caribbean studies showed that it is likely to turn into depression. In China, it was also linked to psychiatric disorders, even when factoring out for genetic traits. Chinese research also showed that these children cannot regulate their emotions as well

It can also interfere with learning—studies show that there is a correlation between authoritarianism and lower school achievement. When children are made to feel fear or shame surrounding poor performance, this doesn't bring about positive results. Rather, they are more likely to struggle with problem-solving and creative tasks, probably because their brains are in a high-adrenaline, fight or flight state so much of the time. Research shows that people actually respond better to positive reinforcement, rather than negative, especially when dealing with children. In San Francisco, one study showed that no matter the ethnic group, children got lower grades when they were parented with authoritarian values. These findings were duplicated over and over. Even within schools themselves, when programs are run with authoritarian teachers and principals, their dropout rates are higher and students achieve at lower levels.

Authoritative Parenting – Positive Reinforcement

<u>Authoritative parenting,</u> on the other hand, has hallmarks of reasonable demands and a high degree of responsiveness. Although authoritative parents have high expectations of their children, they also give them the resources they need to succeed. Parents who exhibit this style of parenting, whether they know the name for it or not, listen to their children and provide love and warmth in addition to setting limits and doling out fair discipline. These parents avoid punishment and threats, instead relying on strategies such as conversation, natural consequences, and positive reinforcement.

In authoritative homes, there is usually fair discipline and consistent consequences for breaking rules, but these are issued with respect. Children can express their opinions and are involved in family discussions, even regarding the discipline itself. Parents are affectionate—physically and verbally—which encourages the children to do the same. Young people are encouraged to be independent and use critical thinking skills. Parents listen to their children and place consequences, expectations, and limits on behavior while still accepting the child as a whole being.

Authoritative homes don't practice things "by the book." They take situations individually, and respond with thought and detail to the situation at hand, taking all variables into account. This also means that this style of parenting doesn't look the same in every family. (This "style" probably has the most variations in positive parenting.) For example, when researchers surveyed parents in four different countries—China, the United States, Russia, and Australia—they found an interesting pattern. In the U.S. and Australia, authoritative parents were very likely to emphasize certain democratic practices, such as taking a child's preferences into account when making family plans, or encouraging a child to express his or her own opinions. In China and Russia, however, authoritative parents didn't take their children's preferences into account when making family plans. Most authoritative parents from China didn't encourage children to voice their own opinions; instead, authoritative styles took a different form.

If not with punishments and threats, then, how do authoritative parents discipline their children? By shaping behavior through reasoning, emotional coaching, and emphasizing empathy and concern for others.

Parenting with warmth and affection is also a good way to prevent children from developing negative behavior traits as they age. Although it's not one-hundred percent for certain, children who were raised with plenty of physical affection, positive affirmation, and gentle, respectful discipline were much less likely to develop low amounts of empathy, low levels of self-regulation, or poor moral choices—even when they carried genetic markers for these traits.

Children who are raised in authoritative homes are confident and believe that they are capable of trying and learning new things. They have solid social skills, heightened emotional control and self-regulation (compared to children from permissive or authoritarian homes), and are overall happier, more positive people.

This all stems from the fact that authoritative parents are good role models for their children, practicing the same behaviors and lifestyle that they expect their young ones to develop. Their children are more likely to develop these positive behaviors because they not only hear them talked about but see them in practice. Consistency (even with flexibility) also helps them know what to expect in a given situation.

Some parents might initially gravitate toward one parenting style or another. However, if you would like to try and become a more authoritative parent to be able to give your child the best foundation for developing into a healthy emotional and social life, it is possible! Here are 12 skills to develop on your way to becoming a more authoritative parent:

1. **Listening to your child** – Children are human beings worthy of respect, and a valuable part of society. It is important to listen to their ideas, concerns, and thoughts—no matter how small or unimportant they may seem to you.
2. **Validating your child's emotions** – Learning emotional intelligence and being able to "name"

emotions is an essential life skill. We all feel things and need to know what those feelings mean.

3. **Considering your child's feelings** – You can be the leader of the home while still thinking about the way your decisions will make your child feel. There's a difference in acknowledging what they are going through and letting them dictate the family decisions.

4. **Establishing clear rules** – Children function best when they know what to expect and what is expected of them. Rules and structure are best understood when there is a "why" behind them so that the child really understands the reasoning behind their choices.

5. **Offering warnings for minor issues** – This prepares a child for what is to come. They might not know that their silly, obnoxious, or negative behavior is unacceptable, but once you give a warning and an intended consequence, make sure to follow through.

6. **Using consequences that teach life lessons** – Natural consequences are the best teachers. If they are sneaking snacks into their room, then those snacks won't be bought again, for example. No need to yell, spank, or threaten. Natural consequences allow you to stay calm and simply say, "That's what happens."

7. **Offering incentives for desired behavior** – These

should also be related to the behavior at hand. For example, when a child is keeping their room clean without being asked, then they are able to accept the responsibility of more grown-up toys in that room.

8. **Allowing your child to make small choices for shared control** – The majority of children's lives are decided for them. This can make them feel as if they have no input. For instance, let them choose if they want carrots or broccoli with dinner—either way, they're eating a vegetable! And you'll have less frustration when they were involved in the choice.

9. **Balancing freedom with responsibility** – Many parents allow their children a lot of freedom as young kids and then tighten up the reins as they get older. This is confusing to an adolescent, as they want more freedom as they grow. Instead, give them firm, appropriate boundaries as small children, and as they show the ability to make good, responsible decisions, allow them more space to roam (literally and figuratively).

10. **Turning mistakes into learning opportunities** – Every poor choice contains a lesson. You want your kids to make mistakes when they're young—and remember the natural consequences—so that they are less likely to make them again when they're older and the consequences are move damaging.

11. **Encouraging self-discipline** – Eventually, children will be out on their own. If you control all their

choices and discipline for them, they'll never know how to do it for themselves. Plus, when young people are encouraged to take responsibility for their own discipline, it's less work for you (in the long run).

12. **Maintaining a healthy relationship with your child** – This simply makes things more positive for everyone involved. Putting in the work and effort in the early years helps ensure that your children will come to you when they're older. Having open, honest communication that is not based around fear will keep them trusting you as a valid authority in their lives.

Permissive and/or Helicopter Parents – Is Indulgent Parenting Bad for Your Child?

Permissive parenting is characterized by low demands of children and high responsiveness from parents. Permissive parents tend to be very loving, yet they provide few guidelines and rules to help their children navigate along the paths of life. These parents do not expect mature behavior from their children, often seeming and acting more like a friend than a parent or authority figure. This style is also often called "indulgent parenting."

Permissive parents usually show great deals of affection to their children, which is good. However, they also use lavish gifts, food treats, and a revolving cycle of new toys or activities as encouragement for what the parent wants or needs.

They allow children to have an equal or majority share in the decisions of the family or home, and put more emphasis on the child's freedom rather than their responsibilities. There is usually no schedule or structure to daily activities, and children simply do whatever they like. Rules and standards of behavior are inconsistent, and parents are usually looked at as more of a friend (oftentimes on purpose).

There are many negative effects of permissive parenting. Children raised in this manner often display low achievement in a variety of areas, make poor decisions, and are prone to delinquency and substance abuse. Since parents don't have high expectations of their children, the kids don't have anything to strive toward, especially if they don't have high levels of intrinsic motivation. These kids often don't do well in school as the parents don't value the structure there, either. Children with permissive parents don't have good practice with problem-solving or decision-making skills, since parents do most of their "learning" for them.

Many children from permissive homes show heightened displays of aggression and less emotional understanding, and they are often susceptible to gang-related behavior and substance abuse. They are also more likely to manage their time unwisely or have a series of bad habits that negatively affect them or others. Permissive parenting doesn't place value on learning to effectively deal with your emotions—oftentimes negative feelings are just swept under the rug and covered with a Band-Aid in the form of treats, food, or material goods. Children from these types of homes don't know what it's like to have limits or the positive effects of self-discipline, so they struggle to limit themselves with things such as food, screen time, or leisure time, which can make coming into their own as adults quite difficult.

If you know that permissive parenting is the style you have fallen into and want to change it, you can do so with some effort and emotional elbow grease. Develop a list of basic household rules and routines. Ensure that whatever "laws" you set down are ones that you are comfortable enforcing and following through with. Make sure your kids are on the same page as you and that they understand the consequences of breaking rules. Reward and notice good behavior.

Some types of permissiveness give children a distinct advantage, however. We need to let children make their own choices and fail in small ways so that they learn from natural consequences. This way, as they age, they will remember the lessons learned when they were young and not have to suffer larger, harder, more serious consequences as young adults.

Uninvolved – Is Neglectful Parenting the Worst Parenting Style?

Uninvolved parenting is characterized by a lack of responsiveness to a child's needs. Uninvolved parents make few to no demands of their children; they are often indifferent, dismissive, or even completely neglectful, ignoring basic needs.

Uninvolved parents do not respond well (or at all) to the needs of their children and provide little affection, support, or love. They also make very few demands of their offspring. They rarely set rules and do not offer guidance or expectations for behavior.

Uninvolved parents often come from dysfunctional families themselves. They may have had uninvolved or neglectful parents as role models and do not know how to lead their family any differently. They also tend to have mental health issues such as depression, anxiety, or substance abuse issues, many times stemming from unresolved childhood trauma.

Signs of uninvolved parents include lack of emotional attachment to one's child, complete focus on their own desires and problems (away from their child's), lack of interest or participation in their child's activities, and/or no set rules or expectations of behavior. Uninvolved parents are so preoccupied with their own lives, that their children's needs are deemed as unimportant. They don't intentionally make time for their children, oftentimes on purpose putting everything before them. Whatever is going on in the child's life, whether it's a parent-teacher conference, a book series the child loves, or a soccer game, is too low on the totem pole for an uninvolved parent. A parent who is uninvolved might not know how to emotionally attach to their child, not having been shown appropriate love and affection during their own formative years. This lack of attachment and lack of desire for involvement is also closely linked with a lack of rules and/or expectations, which would require effort on the part of the parent. These behaviors are often a defense mechanism for something deeper, but it still affects the children in a deeply negative way.

Children of uninvolved parents have a whole host of struggles. They are often anxious or stressed due to the lack of family involvement or support, or are emotionally withdrawn and show a struggle to create attachments or emotionally healthy relationships. They fear becoming dependent on other people and have an increased risk of substance abuse. Children of uninvolved parents learn at a young age that they need to provide for themselves, which can often cause emotional or behavioral syndromes or disorders. They tend to exhibit more signs of delinquency during adolescence, as well.

It is important to distinguish between busy parents and neglectful parents. Almost all parents are busy, whether it is with work commitments inside or outside the home, other children and family commitments, educational responsibilities, community involvement, or often a combination of any of these. Busy parents still choose to spend their free moments connecting with their kids, and carve out time to spend with them and let them know how loved they truly are.

Uninvolved parenting is not necessarily the same as free-range parenting, either; this is a style in which children have a great deal more choice and freedom but with the overarching eye and supervision of their parents. Free-range parents love their children deeply and take great interest in their children's activities and interests. They simply allow their children much more freedom to learn on their own, and help them navigate life with natural rewards and consequences.

SCENARIOS FOR CONCRETE UNDERSTANDING

Read the following situations and take an honest look inside yourself to try and find which ones sound like your home or your style.

Authoritarian

Scenario 1: In the Fernandez home, everything served to you on your plate is eaten, no matter what. Food is a precious resource, and Mom works very hard to cook each night before Dad gets home from work. If you don't like what is on your plate, it doesn't matter—not only will you be made to stay at the table until bedtime, but if you still don't finish your food it will be served to you again for breakfast.

Scenario 2: The Rawlings children must pick up all their toys directly after playing with them. One day, the youngest two kids became engrossed in a game and moved on to another area of the home. Their mother saw the toys left in the backyard and while they were playing in the living room, she got a trash bag and collected all the toys she could see from their bedrooms, the yards, and the common areas. The children saw what she was doing and began crying, trying to explain that they weren't done. She loaded the children into the car and proceeded to drop the trash bags off at the Goodwill, saying, "Maybe next time you'll remember to clean up after yourself."

Authoritative

Scenario 1: Janessa's mother was tired of reminding her 12-year-old daughter to remember what she needed for school each day: homework, lunch, jacket, etc. When expressing this to her, Janessa sighed, "Mom, just leave me alone, I don't need you to remind me about everything." The mother decided to let off the next day and see what happened. Instead of rushing around the house and shouting off the list of each need, she simply asked her daughter if she had everything. When Janessa left and her mother noticed her folder in her bedroom, her jacket by the door, and her lovingly prepared lunch still in the fridge, she took a deep breath resolved to not bring it all to her. Janessa came home hungry from not wanting to eat the unappetizing hot lunch, a bit cold as it was a windy day, and frustrated that her homework would receive a zero. Her mother asked her what she thought they should do to remedy it, and they decided on a checklist by the door that Janessa could go through herself each morning.

Scenario 2: The Henderson family was full of growing boys who loved to eat. Their parents worked hard and enjoyed being able to provide their family with fun, albeit healthy, treats to have around the house. However, they felt like every time they opened the pantry, it was time to go to the grocery store again, even though they knew they were providing adequate amounts of food. Their parents discussed the food budget with the boys, showing them that there was a certain amount of money allotted toward groceries each month. Then they invited the boys on a shopping trip, giving them each $20 to spend on desired snacks for those two weeks. Each boy's choices were put into a particular drawer in the pantry. The parents discussed how much could probably be eaten each day to last, but didn't enforce, remind, or nag when they saw a child overindulging. When, only a few days later, some of the boys' snacks were gone, they simply replied with, "What a bummer. We'll go shopping again next weekend. I know you'll be okay until then."

Permissive

Scenario 1: Sunita had been asking her parents for a dog for quite a while, so for her thirteenth birthday they bought her an eight-week-old Golden Retriever and wrapped a big red bow around his neck. They said, "This is your dog, so you'll have to take care of him!" However, they got up every time the dog needed to go outside, picked up all the poop, and fed the dog when they got up in the morning "because it was just easier to do it themselves." Although Sunita played with and cuddled the puppy often, she would always say she was busy when the dog needed to be walked. When Sunita left her door open and clothes, art supplies, or books on the floor and the dog chewed them up, her parents simply laughed to themselves about how forgetful she was and bought replacements. Sunita left the back gate open one day a few months later and the dog ran out, leading to the parents making and putting up fliers for a lost dog, but it was never found. Sunita cried and cried, and begged for a new pet, which they bought for her "as long as she promised to be more responsible next time."

Scenario 2: Charles was far from an avid student, showing a lack of drive and attention to his schoolwork. His dad remembered being the same way in school and would say, "Look at me, I was never a great student and I turned out fine." Tired of hearing the complaints from his teachers, his mother would sit with him at the table and try to encourage him on his schoolwork, but ended up just giving him the answers and completing projects mostly on her own as it was such a hassle. When his teachers said that he wasn't performing well on tests, Charles' parents told themselves that he was probably distracted in the classroom and asked for assessments to be sent home so that Charles could work in a "quieter environment."

Uninvolved

Scenario 1: Abigail was not planning on having children, as it didn't line up with her timeline for law school and a high-paced career in the courts. However, she unexpectedly became pregnant, but felt that it was a blessing she had such a high-paying job where she could just hire a nanny instead. As years went on, others did all the child-rearing for her. She would get home at the end of the day, her daughter would come to her asking to be read to or played a game with, and Abigail would simply say, "Oh, no, Mommy has more work to do, you can watch a movie," and then retreat to her bedroom with her personal vices. Her daughter always ate alone with whatever the nanny had prepared, and put herself to bed each night. As Abigail's daughter grew, she learned that her mother couldn't be bothered to make time for her, so she searched out relationships elsewhere.

Scenario 2: Adam's mother worked nights at the local casino, while an elderly neighbor watched over him. Adam's mother would return in the wee hours of the morning and sleep until after he had gotten himself up and out the door for school, usually late. Her days were spent with myriad friends and boyfriends that were in and out of their lives like a revolving door. She provided enough cereal, ramen, and peanut butter and jelly to always have something available, but her own meals were eaten on the way to and from work or her various daytime activities. Adam learned to cut moldy crusts off of bread and put water in his cereal if the milk had spoiled. Their home was in shambles, with mail piled up on the counters and the utilities often shut off for unpaid bills. His teachers were concerned about Adam's unkempt appearance, inattention to schoolwork and homework, and his descriptions of his home life. Social services didn't deem the situation neglectful enough to warrant removal from the home, though, so his teachers simply encouraged him as best as they could since they knew from experience that asking his mother for more attention was ineffective.

4

THE EMPATHETIC PARENT

One of the principles of raising a well-behaved child is to teach them empathy and to be empathetic toward their thoughts, feelings, and circumstances. This chapter will guide you through everything you should know about how to raise an empathetic child through modeling empathy yourself.

Relationships that influence an individual's development are characterized by connections; this begins at the moment of birth. Parental empathy is the main characteristic of such relationships, and it shows a real commitment. Physical and emotional availability given to children from the day they are born makes a big difference in developing the proper synapses and "teaching" children the skills they need to become empathetic humans. Early empathetic relationships are vital for healthy development, which is evident in abundant amounts of research.

Studies show that our innate sense of who we are is developed through our relationships with our parents or our primary caregivers. When these relationships are given the attention to develop authentic, true, meaningful connection that has a foundation in empathy and responsiveness, it creates a positive development. When these things are not present, dysfunctional behavior begins to emerge, even into later years of life. The majority of your brain is developed within the first few years of life—about 80%. By age five, 90% of the brain and its synapses are in place. When this early development is characterized by empathetic connections— the ability to share and respect someone else's feelings and perspective—it sets the stage for healthy adult connections. A strong foundation here allows us to have open, accepting relationships and to grow and develop in a way that is safe for all our emotions.

Parental empathy encourages positive development, while its absence is associated with subsequent non-functional patterns of behavior. If parents are insensitive to their children's feelings and needs, it might lead to their kids being frustrated and the parents not understanding what they are experiencing.

HOW TO PARENT WITH MORE EMPATHY

In order to parent with more empathy, you can start by becoming aware of what you tell yourself when your child presents a triggering behavior such as whining or crying. Are you frustrated that your child is not obeying right away? Are you feeling disrespected or upset that you are not in control? Are you anxious that what you want to "get done" might not happen? Identify your foundational feelings so that you can process them.

Then, get out of your head and into your child's—put yourself into their shoes. How might they be feeling? Possibly the same as you? It can be helpful to remember what it was like when you were a child. Did you ever have the same types of experiences? What were the struggles you and your parents had with each other? Ask yourself, "What might my child be feeling in this moment? What do they need from me that I can give them?" This is more effective than "How can I get them to stop crying or whining?"

Become aware of the things your child is saying and their body language, as well as your own feelings. You don't need to be hard on yourself or punish yourself for not having dealt with past situations appropriately, but just notice and make an effort to pay closer attention to your and your child's triggers and responses from now on. A child's upset emotions are not a reflection of you as a parent. It isn't your job to make everything perfect, and life is full of disappointment. You simply are there to help hold space and guide them through the hard times as they learn to self-regulate and learn the deeper workings of the world.

It's also so important for you to take care of yourself. You cannot give from an empty cup, and you are just as important as everyone else in your family. Especially if you're the primary caregiver, or if you work full-time outside the home and are expected to come home and take the lion's share of the childrearing and/or household work... that's a lot of pressure as well as physical, emotional, and mental energy that is going out. Self-care doesn't have to mean spa days and brunches with friends, either. It could simply mean getting up 15 minutes earlier to stretch, meditate, or drink your hot coffee in peace. (We will explore this further in Chapter 7.)

Encourage a solution that works for both of you by helping your child to identify and name their feelings and the true root of the problem for both of you. Allow each other to see where the other is coming from. Do all of this while staying calm—this is of the utmost importance. Your child will mirror the emotions and responses that you are having—if you get upset, angry, and highly emotional, they will do the same (and vice versa if you stay calm). Explain your feelings and the reasoning behind them, naming your emotions. Then guide them in doing the same. Encouraging a solution works best when the solution comes from the child themselves, but, especially in the beginning, they might need help coming up with ideas. As the parent you can offer a few different solutions and let them choose which one they feel most comfortable with.

It is important to create a culture in which your child can express all the emotions they are having. Emotions aren't good or bad—what we do with them can be depending on whether it brings positive or negative ripple effects to us and those around us. The word "empath" means to be able to feel and understand other people's emotions. These people can also see how others might visualize them—which can be difficult as a child when they think you, as the parent, "see" them as bad, annoying, or a burden. Empathy is a positive trait, however, and can be cultivated so that both parent and child have the skills to lovingly respond, relate well with others, anticipate what people are feeling, give words to their thoughts and feelings, and to anticipate the responses and needs of others in our lives.

It also makes a big difference when you can respond to your child's physical hurts with empathy. Oftentimes kids are brushed off with comments such as, "Oh, you're not bleeding," "I don't see a scrape," or "I'm sure you're fine." The truth is, you don't know how your child's body is feeling when something happens to upset them. If they are projecting emotional pain into physical, they are asking for attention either way and looking to you for some sort of affirmation.

Many parents have the initial reaction to a conflict with their child to simply say, "Because I'm the parent" or "Because I said so." However, as children need us to teach them, and they learn through examples, mistakes, and experiences, the best way for them to become empathetic is to explain your choices in decisions, honor their feelings, and to also explain when you are exhibiting empathy to them or others.

HOW TO CULTIVATE EMPATHY IN YOUR CHILD

Although a parent who is well attuned to the needs of their child is one of the steps to creating a beautiful connection, your child needs to meet you halfway. That is why teaching your kids to be empathetic is key to positive behavior and strong emotional control.

You can cultivate an empathetic culture in your home and family by implementing some of these strategies:

- **Teach children how to manage to identify and manage their positive and negative emotions** – To do this, we can practice positive, respectful parenting and use sensitive approaches to discipline that help our children feel secure. We also need to teach our children how to constructively respond to their negative emotions, because they will be present in all of life. There are options to either push them down and ignore them, lash out in anger or resentment, or process and respond in grace.
- **Understand how feelings of guilt and shame can affect a child's empathetic responses** – When children are "the bad guy," or a situation is their fault,

they tend to respond in a way that isn't constructive or helpful because they are feeling ashamed. Accepting shame leads to feeling helpless, sulking, or removing ourselves from the situation. Shame is different than guilt, though. A child can learn to see that they caused a situation and take responsibility, without feeling like they are a bad person. Consequences do not have to equal shame.

- **Seize everyday opportunities to switch on your child's "empathy mode"** – This simply means asking your child what they think others might be feeling, or what they would do or feel in a particular situation.

- **Help kids discover what they have in common with other people** – When children can see that they are similar to others, and that someone who is struggling might have something in common with them, then they are more likely to want to help that person.

- **Don't shelter your child from discussions about intense, sensitive subjects such as race, inequality, and injustice. Talk openly about biases and opinions, facts, and generalizations** – Many parents, especially white parents, feel that they should teach their children to be "color blind," or to live as if racial separations and biases don't exist. However, whether we talk about it openly or stay silent, children still pick up racial biases from culture and interactions. Research also shows that white children in particular have less of a racial bias when their parents hold open conversations about racism.

- **Make perspective-taking an important part of your discussions, and use through practice exercises and group discussion to nurture it –** This is called "cognitive empathy." It involves being able to imagine what someone else is going through or what they need, even if we haven't been in that situation before. Emotion coaching helps, as well as playing games and activities that focus on emotions. Using books for story talk exercises is also effective.

- **Use compassion training to foster empathy –** Compassion meditation involves visualizing certain affirmations, such as being filled with peace, being safe, and being free from suffering. Then, children can think these positive thoughts toward others.

- **Help children develop a sense of morality that depends on internal self-control, not on external rewards and punishments –** Punitive discipline actually encourages children to lie or deceive so that they don't receive punishment. Children should be taught to regulate their emotions and make choices from their inner conscience if we want these lessons to last a lifetime. This is done by talking about how our actions and responses actually affect other people.

- **Talk with children about the rationalizations that**

people use to justify callous or cruel acts and the realities associated with standing up to this (both positive and negative) – There is a great deal of research to show that the average well-adjusted human can be convinced into harming someone else —even severely—if they are given reasons that seem to make sense. They need to know that when they see something happening, they have the power—and responsibility—to do something about it. Oftentimes, too, it means teaching that if they aren't part of a solution they are part of the problem.

- **Empathize with your child and model empathy for others** – Empathy takes practice. The best way to teach your child to have empathy for others is to empathize with them, and put words to the situation. You can also discuss when you are responding in empathy to others, so they can see you using these skills in the world outside your family, which makes it safe for them to do so as well.

- **Make caring for others a priority and set high ethical expectations** – Children emulate what they see their parents doing. When they see you helping, thinking about others besides yourself, and speaking about your moral compass, they will take the same path as they grow.

- **Provide opportunities for children to practice empathy** – These can range from real-life experiences to games, books, and pretend play in which children can practice using the words and actions they are learning. You can role play positive and negative responses to situations, which will help children be confident in using their new skills in myriad situations.

- **Expand your child's circle of concern** – This doesn't necessarily mean watching the nightly news with your four-year-old, but it could mean watching child-appropriate videos of world events, picking out news articles or clips that help them understand what is going on outside their home, and participating in family service projects to help others in their community.

- **Help children develop self-control and teach them resources to manage their feelings effectively** – Self-control is a journey, not a destination. All people need a toolbox of skills to use in different situations and when different feelings emerge. The more they have talked with you about these things, the more comfortable they will feel coming to you when a new situation causes them to stop and think about what they need to do to help another person.

SITUATIONS FOR CONCRETE UNDERSTANDING – USING EMPATHY AND WHEN EMPATHY DOESN'T "WORK"

Using empathy is a practice. The more you use it, the easier you will feel it coming to you as a natural reaction. However, there are often challenges that parents and caregivers face when implementing some of these strategies to teach empathy. There are, thankfully, additional strategies you can use when an obstacle seems to get in the way of the good work you're trying to do.

Putting Yourself into Your Child's Shoes

As an adult, we often forget what a big, scary world this is when we don't have all the resources, opportunities, and knowledge that we have acquired over the years. Goodness —sometimes it is a big and scary world even with all those things! Putting yourself in your child's place can help make sure that you are using your own empathy skills to help them.

Scenario: Jessica's daughter Emma had a serious aversion to having her hair washed. She would cry and scream, saying that the water was getting in her eyes and she was afraid of the "tear-free" shampoo. Jessica kept reminding her that it didn't hurt and she would be fine, but it wasn't working. One day, she wondered what it really felt like. She asked her husband to wash her hair with her eyes shut tight, and realized that it did seem a little anxiety-inducing when she didn't know when he was going to do something or to not have control over where the water was going on her face. When she moved unexpectedly and the "tear-free" shampoo got in her eyes, it was definitely irritating! Jessica apologized to her daughter, and decided to role-play with a new curved cup that molded to her head. She let her daughter wash her hair, and asked her to "Tell mama what you're going to do so I don't get nervous." Jessica used the experience to help Emma practice some vocabulary, saying, "I'm wondering how many times you'll rinse my hair. Could we count? My eyes are closed, where is the cup? Can you tell me when you'll put it on my head?" Then she encouraged Emma to practice on some bath toys as well, and listened to the things she was saying while playing "pretend."

When Empathy Makes My Child Cry Harder

Sometimes, getting down on your child's level and acknowledging the feelings they are having can bring up even bigger emotions. These feelings, however, aren't "created" by you acknowledging them and showing empathy. Imagine how you feel when you have had a really hard day, everything has gone wrong, and you've been holding it together because you have to. Then someone with whom you feel safe gives you a hug and asks you how your day was. You break down and let it all out, because it feels okay in that moment.

Scenario: Kyla comes out of the school building and her mother sees that she is a bit closed off, answering questions with one-word responses and turning her head toward the window of the car. Her mother sees a single tear start to fall down her cheek and her mom says, "I know, sometimes some days are like that." Kyla chin starts quivering and says, "I don't want to talk about it, Mom." Her mother replies with a gentle, "It's okay. I'm here if you need me," and gently brushes her daughter's hair back behind her ear. Kyla buries her face in her hands and begins sobbing uncontrollably. Her mother listens (without trying to solve or lessen her daughter's problems), and, when appropriate, responds with comments such as, "That sounds hard to deal with... How did that make you feel?... Wow, was that scary?... That must have been overwhelming." These comments open Kyla up to speaking more deeply and are calming at the same time.

When Empathy Doesn't Stop the Tantrum

You might be empathizing with your child; however, their tantrum continues without any signs of tempering! Sometimes children need to show their heavy, hard emotions before healing can take place. Again, your job is not to stop the emotions. It is to give acceptance, communicate a safe space, and let your child know that their feelings are okay. In a situation like this, less is more (with regard to words).

Scenario: Four-year-old AJ comes storming in from the yard, where he had been playing with his siblings. "No one wants to play with me and they're all stupid and I hate that game!" His dad sees the frustration and anger in his face and in his body language, so he stops and tells himself that this will best be handled with a calm demeanor. He gets down on AJ's level and says, "I hear you, buddy. Do you want to tell me what happened?" AJ looks at his father, scrunches up his face, sucks in a huge breath, and shouts at the top of his lungs while stomping up and down. His father knows that he needs to let these feelings out, so he asks if AJ would like a hug. "NO! I just want to make them all go away forever!" His father decides to just name his response. "You were all playing and things didn't work out, and now you're angry because that's one of your favorite games." His son looks at him and says, with all the emotion of a betrayed child, and says, "YES. They told me I can't play with them anymore because I'm too little and they only want big kids. I wish I was so big I could *step on them all!*" His father simply takes a deep breath and says, "I know, AJ. It's so hard when people we love don't treat us in a kind way. Would you like my help talking to them or would you like to do something special with Dad instead? Or you can go next door and see if the neighbors can play." AJ simply stomps away, saying, "I don't like you either!" His dad knows that he can leave him be, and he will come back in a little while having calmed down with the knowledge that his feelings were accepted.

When You Empathize but They Are Still Upset

Remember, your job is not to "fix," but to be compassionate. It's okay to be upset! Children should be given the freedom to feel the feelings that they feel. When they can learn this as a child, it makes it much easier to deal with the same types of situations as an adult. Learning resilience is crucial to a healthy emotional life as an adult. Sometimes, however, taking this a step further and helping come up with a solution can bring them out of the emotional state of mind and into a new idea.

Scenario: Sophia and her parents are at the mall shopping for new school shoes, when they pass by the toy store and there is an elaborate display of the newest dolls in the fad trend. She stops abruptly, "MOM. DAD. All the girls in my class have those dolls. I want one soooo bad! Can we go in and get one pleeeeaaaase??" The parents look at each other and sigh, "Oh, Sophia, those are beautiful dolls! We've seen them on the commercials. But today we are only here for school shoes, that's all we have the budget for this month." She looks at them with tears in her eyes. "But, everyone else has them and I've been wanting them foreeeeever!!" They kneel down next to her. "We know. There are things we want that we see other grown-ups have, too. But there just isn't money for it right now. Can you think of a way to help save for a new doll?" Sophia replies, "Save? For how long?" Mom takes a deep breath, "Well, let's go in and check to see how much the doll is. You get your allowance every week, we can make a chart to see how long it would take to save." Sophia eyes her warily. "What about for my birthday?" Mom smiles, "Yes, that's coming up soon, too! Would you like to put it on your birthday list and then maybe save some of your own money for some doll clothes?" Sophia takes a deep breath. "Okay…" She looks back sadly as they walk away, but her parents know they are beginning to teach a valuable lesson.

When Your Words Make Your Child Angry and They Tell You to Stop

Many children are initially uncomfortable with hearing their emotions identified. Especially as older children and adolescents, sometimes hearing their emotions named can make them feel manipulated and micro-managed instead of understood. Here is a place where it is important to know your child. How do they best feel seen, heard, and acknowledged? If they're already past the point of learning to name their emotions, then simply responding in an accepting and understanding way can do the trick.

Scenario: Bran runs off the soccer field after having missed the last penalty shot which would have won his team the game. He is close to tears, and his face is a storm cloud of emotion. His parents open their arms to hug him, but he turns away. "I'm the lousiest soccer player there ever was!" They say gently, "No, you're not, Bran! You're a great soccer player! No one makes every goal." He glares at them. "Some people do! I could have made that shot and I didn't!" They reply with, "Yes, but it's okay, you're still an important team member and you've worked so hard…" He turns away from them, "You don't hear me, I didn't do it and I knew I could! I wanted to win and I lost it!" They sigh, and say, "You're right. Can we try again? It's so frustrating to feel like something is so close and it didn't happen, especially when it was in your control. It makes you wish you could go back and do it all again but you can't. That disappointment is hard to sit with." Bran looks at them, eyes narrowed still but less anger in his voice when he says, "Yeah. Something like that. Can we just go home?" They put their arms around him. "Yep, let's go get you in a hot shower and you can choose what you want for dinner."

When You Redirect but the Behavior Happens Again Right Afterward

Behaviors often take many, many repetitions to break a bad habit and learn another positive behavior. Oftentimes, when parents are trying to acknowledge and also change behavior, they use the word 'but.' For example, "I know you're really angry that your brother knocked down your tower, but we don't hit each other." However, this can make a child feel that they aren't truly acknowledged in their experience. Using the word 'and' is more productive. It's also important to remember that talking alone doesn't change behavior—practice, repetition of appropriate choices, and a safe space do.

Scenario: Lanie's two-year-old sister Annie comes into her room and picks up some LEGOs, trying to push them into place. The construction that Lanie had been working on for about an hour comes crashing down. "Moooooooom! Annie get out! You ruin everything!" She pushes her down and then tries to push her out of the bedroom. Lanie's mom sighs and walks calmly into the room, thinking, "Will this ever stop?" She has talked to Lanie about this seemingly over and over but it keeps happening. Their mother says, "Lanie, let me go set Annie up with something in her room and I'll be right back." She returns after giving Annie a snack and her own blocks and says, "How long were you working on that? What was it going to be?" Lanie cries, "A castle! I'd been working on it all day!" Mom replies, "Gosh, that's so frustrating. I know this has been happening a lot and I'm sorry. Annie just wants to be with you." Lanie says, "I know, but I just want to do it by myself!" Mom stops and looks at her. "You're right. Sometimes having a little sister isn't all fun. You deserve to have your own space. What if you let me know when you plan on doing something where you don't want to be interrupted, and you can use my room and shut the door?" Lanie's eyes light up, knowing that it's a special offer. "Wow, thanks, Mom. Okay… I guess I can go play with her blocks with her for a little while." Lanie has felt heard and given something special for her own, so feels less pressured to force this time by pushing her sister out.

5

FOSTER AN EMOTIONAL CONNECTION

Positive relationships between parents and children are important for all areas of children's development. This chapter explores important strategies that parents can use to connect with their kids emotionally as well as what they can do at every developmental stage to ensure they maintain positive relationships with their children into adolescence and beyond. Children who have healthy relationships with their parents become parents who create healthy relationships with their own families. It might seem like a mountainous task to break the cycles of your own upbringing, but it has to start somewhere. Why not with you?

WHY DO EMOTIONAL TIES BETWEEN KIDS AND THEIR PARENTS MATTER?

The feeling that binds us to the significant people in our lives is known as attachment. The term "attach" means to tie, fasten, or connect one thing to another. The attachment relationship between a parent and a child is a lot like a rope —every positive interaction between a parent and their offspring adds a new thread and strengthens the overall emotional connection.

There are four types of attachment: secure, avoidant, ambivalent, and unorganized. (These are the four types that have been identified and studied—there may be more, or combinations of the various styles.) Each one is caused— whether you like it or not—by the choices you make in infancy and early childhood with regard to your relation-ships with your children.

A Note on Cultural Differences: Depending on the country and culture, caregivers show love and affection in different ways. Adults can always build secure attachment through showing sensi-tivity and response to a child's needs, no matter the way they give these responses. If you work with children and families from many different cultures (especially ones that differ from your own) be sure to educate yourself.

Secure Relationships

When children are securely, emotionally attached to people who care for them, they receive valuable support that helps them to grow and develop. Secure relationships (when children feel safe with their parents or caregivers and believe they will be taken care of) foster emotionally healthy human beings.

How Children and Adults with Secure Attachments Behave

Children who show secure attachment usually or often:

- Play well with other children their age.
- Cry when their parent leaves (during infancy, toddlerhood, and preschool age) but then calm down easily with a safe adult to comfort them.
- React with happiness when a parent comes to pick them up.
- Might sometimes still have a hard time leaving childcare or school.

Adults who foster secure attachments usually or often:

- Consistently respond to their child's needs.
- Respond with love and attention when their child cries.
- Feed their child in a timely manner when they cry.

- Take care of the child when they are afraid.
- Show shared excitement when the child is excited about something.

Avoidant Relationships

When children develop this type of attachment to their parents, they are insecure because their parents aren't responsive to their needs. They never know if someone is going to pay attention to or deliver what they need, so they put up walls (even if that isn't what they realize they're doing) and learn to "not care."

How Children and Adults with Avoidant Attachments Behave

Children who show avoidant attachments usually or often:

- Are more independent than is developmentally appropriate.
- Don't seek out help, but are easily frustrated.
- Have difficulty connecting with same-age peers.
- Show aggressive behavior such as biting, pushing, hitting, or screaming (more than is normal for their developmental age group).
- Do not form solid relationships with secondary caregivers.
- Seem nonchalant both about being dropped off and picked up. They almost seem to "ignore" on purpose.

Adults who foster avoidant attachments usually or often:

- Respond to their child's needs, but on the parent's timetable (which often takes a while).
- Feed their children adequately, but usually after a great time has passed since the child showed signs of hunger.
- Leave their children to deal with fears and anxieties on their own.
- Ignore or dismiss their child's excitement.

Ambivalent Relationships

Here, the needs of the child are sometimes met, but not always, and never with consistency. The child is confused and frustrated, often exhibiting signs of fear or anxiety when a parent leaves because they don't know if they will be back or not.

How Children and Adults with Ambivalent Attachments Behave

Children who show ambivalent attachments usually or often:

- Cling with great need to their caregiver(s).
- Have heightened displays of emotion.
- Act younger than they actually are.

- Try to be the center of attention with crying, frustration, or dramatic antics.
- Have a hard time playing independently.
- Latch on to particular people for short periods.
- Have a difficult time when their parents leave, often crying for long periods.

Adults who foster ambivalent attachments usually or often:

- Respond to crying sometimes, but sometimes not.
- Sometimes feed a child when they are hungry, but often offer food when no signs of hunger are present.
- Do not offer comfort for fears and anxieties with any consistency.
- Doesn't respond to their child's excitement with appropriate levels of their own, or doesn't try to understand why they are excited.

Disorganized Attachments

In this type of emotional development, parents often neglect the child's needs and the child doesn't ever know what to expect from their "safe" adults. Sometimes needs are met, but not usually, and when needs are met they are matched with unfitting responses. Disorganized relationships often happen in families with neglect, abuse, addiction, or mental health disorders.

Children with disorganized attachments are categorized into two types: controlling-disorganized and caregiving-disorganized. Children who are controlling-disorganized are often extremely bossy, try to control the play, and get frustrated when others don't succumb to their wishes or desires. Children who are caregiving-disorganized treat other children as younger than them, and try to be the "grown-up" in all situations. They might seem to care for others, but in a way that is too much.

Children who show disorganized attachments usually or often:

- React to situations or play in ways that do not make logical sense.
- Speak very quickly and are difficult to understand.
- Stop and freeze, seemingly not knowing what to do next.
- Have a difficult time empathizing with others.
- Act out scenes in their play that are scary, confusing, or full of anxiety.
- Act differently from day to day.

Adults who foster disorganized attachments usually or often:

- Rarely respond to their baby's needs and/or cries.
- Respond with an inappropriate level for the situation or need.

BEGINNING IN INFANCY

As stated above, the best time to develop these secure attachments is in infancy. This is done in a variety of ways, easily remembered as "The Seven B's" by Dr. Sears.

- **Birth bonding** – A close attachment and secure relationship begins its roots directly after birth, and can be fostered with skin-to-skin connection, staying with your baby in your room (instead of a nursery), and beginning to be sensitive to baby's needs from the get-go. However, this isn't a "one and done" situation. If something happens to prevent bonding from the first hours and/or days, it can still be developed.
- **Breastfeeding or feeding with high levels of emotional contact** – Breastfeeding is the natural, normal way that humans were meant to be fed, and it naturally fosters skin-to-skin connection, high levels of eye contact, and a need for baby and mom to be near each other at all times. However, this isn't always possible or easy in modern society, so no matter how you choose to feed your child, simply make sure they are talked to, held gently, and that their hunger cues are responded to appropriately.
- **Babywearing** – Wearing your baby in a sling or carrier helps you keep them close so you can be aware of their cues, feed them on demand, and allow

them to sleep easily next to your scent, heartbeat, and warmth. There are many ways this can be done to ensure the safety, comfort, and ease of movement for both parent and child.

- **Bedsharing or co-sleeping** – Humans have been sleeping near their children from the beginning of their existence—how else would early humans have kept their children safe? Both bedsharing or "room sharing" allow you to be close enough to hear baby's cries and attend to their needs quickly—and easily— so that everyone can get the rest they need.

- **Belief in your baby's cues/cries** – Babies do not manipulate. They tell you what they need, when they need it. Crying is a late sign of need! If you learn to recognize your baby's *cues* early on, then things usually go much more smoothly and there is less crying to deal with from the beginning. However, sometimes there just isn't a way to get them to stop crying, and in that case, your job isn't to stop it, but to be there for them with comfort and a safe place.

- **Beware of 'baby trainers'** — Infancy (and often toddlerhood) have a high level of need for "nighttime parenting" as well as meeting your child's many needs during the rest of the day. This is exhausting for many parents, especially in today's society, which isn't built around that "village" humans were designed to have. However, baby trainers don't make your child's needs go away, they simply "train" your baby to learn to need you less. This might seem to be a positive thing, until the negative effects are seen later in life.

- **Balance** – Everything seems easier on paper, and then real life hits. Every child is different, every family dynamic has its own kinks and quirks. No one knows what is best for your baby and your family better than you. Listen to your instinct, find what works for you, and leave the rest behind. If you are reading this, and are actively trying to create a loving, safe, secure place for your child, then all will probably fall into a pretty okay place. Perfect isn't attainable, so don't try. Just give it your best, and that will be enough.

If you are out of the infancy stages of childhood, but reading this makes you wish you could go back and do things differently, it's not too late! Each and every one of these "Bs" is something that you can take and apply to later childhood or even adolescence to help develop strong emotional bonds with your child.

PARENT-CHILD RELATIONSHIP AT VARIOUS STAGES

Depending on the stage of development, there are specific ways your child is growing and learning, and thus, specific ways that you can help them grow healthfully.

Infancy

This is an important time for building warmth and security between child and parent. Research shows that how well an infant is attached to their primary caregiver usually influences the level of health in their later development and relationships. Oftentimes, infants who have a happier, more go-with-the-flow temperament are easier to form a secure attachment with. If the caregiver realizes this, though, and seeks out help and support with a baby that is colicky, high-need, or has other issues that create a difficult situation, then they can still work toward creating a secure attachment.

Toddlerhood

During this time, your child is learning to step out of the family unit and into society, but still needs you as a "home base." Since the relationship isn't so much focused on survival needs at this point, the parent becomes a type of "teacher" about the world and helps the toddler to socialize. The relationship is often concerned with how responsive and/or demanding the parent is at this stage of the child's life. Usually, parents who are responsive, warm, affectionate, and caring foster a healthy development. When parents exhibit low levels of responsiveness, are overly critical, show little enjoyment of their children, or place demands that are too high or too low for their child's developmental age, it begins to cause disconnect and insecurity.

Assertiveness on the child's part during this stage is normal as they are learning to do things on their own and grow into themselves. Parents and caregivers should remember that this assertiveness is a sign of healthy growth and development.

Preschool

These years bring a great deal of learning and growth, as well as influence from the outside world. Many parents feel that this is the time when they feel internal or external pressure to choose a "parenting style." Healthy parent-child relationships are usually characterized by authoritative parents —those who deal with their children with firm rules and discipline but also large amounts of affection, empathy, and grace. Parents who are authoritarian (overly demanding and strict), indulgent (too lenient with few expectations) or uninvolved (neglectful or unaware of the child's needs) foster unhealthy development.

School Age

When a child is between the ages of 5 and 12, they begin understanding the depth of knowledge available about the world beyond their home. They need you for guidance as they are deciding who they are and what they believe. During this time, children begin forming strong relationships with their peers, but that doesn't mean that they need to pull away from their parents. On the contrary, it is even more important now for parents to keep up a healthy, open, secure attachment with their children so that the child's sense of self and "safe place" is in the home, not in the world at large.

Adolescence

Children are becoming young adults during the adolescent years, and they not only need personal space to become who they are, but support from their parents that they are good, capable, intelligent, and kind, no matter the choices they make. During this time, the child is obviously going through significant physical, mental, and emotional changes. If the work has been done in the formative years, this stage is easier. However, the teenager's sense of need for individuation might be frightening or anxiety-inducing to the parent, leading to conflict and push back on both sides. Adolescents need to feel that their independence is accepted, though, and the family dynamics fare best with support from parents in this growth.

Young Adulthood

Now your child is ready for a relationship with you on equal footing, so to speak. Adults soon need to begin looking after their own children or facing their own demands of a life apart from their parents; with a safe and secure attachment, they will know that they can always find a secure support system at home.

PRINCIPLES OF A PARENT-CHILD RELATIONSHIP

There is no "one-size-fits-all" style with regard to parenting. However, these principles lay the foundation for positive parenting that develops healthy emotional relationships.

- Set parenting goals.
- Ground rules are a must.
- Interact with warmth and structure.
- Acknowledge and empathize with your child.
- Use problem-solving skills when approaching conflict.

HABITS TO STRENGTHEN A PARENT-CHILD RELATIONSHIP

If you can implement all—or even most—of these into your regular interactions with your child, then you're off on a good foot to a relationship that will bring you both joy for many years to come.

- Aim for 12+ hugs or physical connections every day.
- Play with your children at their level.
- Connect before transitioning.

- Turn off technology when you interact with your child.
- Welcome emotion and model it yourself.
- Make quality one-on-one time a priority.
- Listen and empathize with their feelings and experiences.
- Slow down and savor the small, ordinary moments.
- Show up when they need you.
- Prioritize bedtime snuggles and daily check-ins.

SCENARIOS FOR CONCRETE UNDERSTANDING

Depending on the relationship you have developed with your child and how they grew to understand the world during their formative years, they may exhibit any of the four types of attachment. Sometimes, their attachment needs may be a factor in difficult behavior.

Children with Secure Attachments

Scenario: Annabelle's pregnancy with her first child was uneventful and easy, and she read everything she could get her hands on. However, beginning with the birth, things began taking their own course. Annabelle ended up needing a Cesarean because of unwanted hospital interventions, and then struggled to breastfeed without adequate support. Although these were disappointments to her, she knew from her reading that the most important element was the love and attention she showed to her baby each day. She wore her son, Jakeem, in a sling while doing her daily tasks and errands, and kept him either next to her in bed or in a bedside bassinet. Annabelle didn't have much support from family, and needed to work, but she asked her boss if she could bring Jakeem to work two or three times a week to spend more time with him—using babywearing as a way to still get her work tasks done with him sleeping for long periods in the carrier. When he did have to go to daycare, she chose a small in-home facility that allowed Jakeem to still get the attention he needed. He cried often when she left, but perked up quickly and was always happy upon her return. As he grew, Jakeem enjoyed school but even more enjoyed the moments when his mama was waiting for him in the afternoons. They walked home together, talking about his day and sharing special moments. Even when stages of Jakeem's life weren't easy, Annabelle took them in stride and leaned on the love she had for her child—and she always sought out help from her community or gathered the resources she needed when she didn't know what to do.

Children with Avoidant Attachments

Scenario: Sebastian's parents were high-profile, hard-working, reach-for-the-stars types who prized their careers above all else. Although they loved their son, they hadn't had parents who were affectionate and involved, and it made them uncomfortable to have a child that seemed to need them so much. They sought out the most expensive daycare/school available and made sure that Sebastian always had all the newest, nicest clothes, toys, and extra-curricular offerings. However, his care was always pushed off to others, and he even had periods where he confusedly thought his nanny was actually his mother. Sebastian was always hailed by teachers and coaches as "fiercely indepen-dent," but he would push to be better than everyone else, always trying to get his parents' attention in some way, shape, or form.

Children with Ambivalent Attachments

Scenario: Janessa's parents had had dysfunctional family relationships themselves, and although they vowed to each other to do better, they didn't quite know how. Her mother read every baby book on the market, and changed her way of disciplining, feeding, sleeping, and caring for Janessa at every turn of the dice. Janessa's father was frustrated by this constant upheaval of what was "supposed" to be happening in the house, and he just did his own thing, which usually conflicted with what Janessa's mother wanted. This caused a great deal of conflict and strife, and Janessa began showing behavioral tendencies of regression into babyish personality traits. She would over-dramatize events, always crying or screaming at the drop of a hat. She began making up imagi-nary friends and would tell tall tales at school that began to cause trouble between her and the other children. Janessa would try to make every new child or substitute teacher her "best friend," and would become very upset if she wasn't the one who could be the ringleader of activities. This was exhausting for her parents, who began to simply ignore the behavior and pacify Janessa with television, food, and new discipline techniques that petered out after a few months, so that Janessa knew she never had to take it all seriously. She rebelled quite a bit as an adolescent, knowing that it was the best way to get attention and that it would be interesting to see how her parents would react, but felt confident that the consequences would never be severe enough to change her behavior.

Children with Disorganized Attachment

Scenario: Dennis was born to parents who weren't fit to take care of him, physically or emotionally. They were a couple who both had substance abuse and mental health issues, and although they tried to care for him for months after his birth, it was a roller coaster and although when his parents were having good weeks of trying to stay clean and healthy, they would care for him as best they could, they continued to fall off the wagon and Dennis was often neglected, forgotten about, or left to cry for hours on end. Around his second birthday, social services took over and he was placed in the foster care system. He went through a series of about a dozen homes before his eighteenth birthday, some with caring, loving parents and foster siblings, and some in which the adults were only participating so that they could receive the support check from the government. Dennis was a very confused boy and often showed aggression or withdrawal with peers and adults, depending on the situation. His drawings, pretend play, and interactions with peers were usually colored with sad, negative, and traumatic events. He knew how to care for himself but didn't seem to have any desire to exhibit positive qualities with regard to hygiene, academic success, or friendships. He brushed everything off with a "whatever" type of attitude, and was seen as a loner during his entire time in school.

6

LOVING THE "DIFFICULT" CHILD

The best and most important gift a parent can give their child is love. Raising a seemingly problematic child is not easy on a parent because they might not instinctively know how to love them in the "best way" for the child's high level of need, or the child's behavior might trigger unprocessed trauma from the parent's own life. This chapter will give you some concrete skills to help you love your child unconditionally—and love yourself unconditionally, too, even when you might mess up.

It's easy to develop a resentful attitude toward a difficult child because they take so much out of you (physically, mentally, emotionally, and spiritually), and because they demand so much more time and energy than either the rest of your children or other children you see out in the world.

If you don't guard your thoughts, you might dwell too much on the negatives of parenting a high-need child. These negative thoughts can in turn affect your heart and the way you view your child as a human as well as the potential for your relationship down the road.

HOW TO LOVE KIDS WHEN THINGS ARE GOOD

Let's start with the "good times" because those are the easiest. Good parenting is not all about discipline for negative or inappropriate behavior—it also involves praising children and noticing when they do the right thing. Parents should avoid giving more praise for some types of positive actions and less praise for others. For example, you shouldn't only congratulate your child when they win a race, but also for simply participating and finishing. That way, you make it clear that success is not the end goal, but rather the effort your child puts into accomplishing something.

When giving praise, focus on comments that reflect the child's accomplishments, such as, "You did it! How do you feel after finishing the race?"

LOVING THROUGH THE BAD TIMES

No matter what is happening, it's important to practice the art of unconditional love. Unconditional love is not a soft, sentimental emotion. It is an intentional choice to relate to a child in a way that separates them from their behavior.

There is a big difference in loving a child when they are doing something negative or harmful and accepting or tolerating that behavior.

Ways to Show Unconditional Love

These are some practical strategies that can be implemented even when you and your child are struggling to see eye-to-eye or they are having a hard time learning what is acceptable in your family culture.

- Play and have fun together in a new space away from the conflict.
- Exhibit small gestures that reflect their love language.
- Include children in family decisions—large and small.
- Maintain flexible structure in the home.
- Treat all children fairly with regard to their individual needs.
- Appreciate the differences in family dynamics.
- Understand that material goods don't equate to love.
- Support your child even when they make mistakes.
- Appreciate your child's weaknesses.
- Grieve together over individual or shared losses.
- See your child's "faults" from their point of view.
- Accept feelings and limit behavior.
- Manage your own anger to be a positive role model.

- Set clear expectations and consequences.
- Give age-appropriate responsibilities so that your child feels needed.

HOW PARENTS CAN FUEL NEGATIVE BEHAVIOR

Every parent *wants* to raise obedient, well-behaved, empathetic, loving, respectful, intelligent children. Unfortunately, though, this isn't always the case. This section will help you understand how your own actions and words might fuel misbehavior in your children.

Not Being Consistent

Why does consistency matter? Consistency is connected to how you connect with your child on an emotional level and the dynamic of your whole family operations. When you are consistent, it means that you intentionally choose how to respond, even when it isn't the easiest choice. Consistent boundaries, structure, and limits also give children a safe space in which to grow, learn, and experiment. Even though children will push against these boundaries, it is good to hold strong, as they want to know how strong those boundaries are.

Inconsistency means that children don't know what will happen from one situation to the next. This can mean they will develop hostile, aggressive, or anxious behavior. It can feel exhausting to think that you have to respond perfectly or in the exact same way each time, but this isn't necessary. You simply need to make an effort to create a home in which things usually happen in the same way with the same type of circumstances. The effort, patience, and time it takes to develop these habits pay off exponentially in the long run.

Failure to Get their Attention

Your child might not be "listening to you" simply because they don't take you seriously. It could also be a case of you saying too much so they filter out your words as "fluff." Children also struggle to focus on more than one thing at a time, so if they are engaged in another activity and you are talking to them without getting their full attention, they might not process what you're saying.

It's important to get down to your child's level and make sure that you are the one they are focused on if what you are saying is important and needs a response. You can also model good listening behavior by not filtering out their own words to you, and listening to them the first time they say or ask something. Look at the situation and think about why they might "not be listening." Stay calm, explain that to hear and not respond appropriately is disrespectful, and take the opportunity to lighten it up and have some fun by making things into a game, setting timers, or engaging in clean-up races. Be patient, too—learning to listen and communicate takes time; haven't you come across many adults who still need practice with these skills?

Excuses

Put an end to your child's excuses by refusing to accept them. Children need to know that they are responsible for their actions and that there are consequences, but this doesn't mean that punishment and shame have to be a part of the lesson. You can stay calm, refuse to engage in power struggles, encourage—and model—personal responsibility, and teach ways to solve problems. Each opportunity can emphasize that there are lessons to be learned from each mistake and that this is how we grow.

Yelling

Believe it or not, there are many ways to exhibit effective discipline without yelling. Yelling comes naturally to many parents, probably because they were yelled at as kids or not taught to manage their own emotions well. Plus, there's only so much defiance and pushback that we can take. However, yelling is shown again and again to be an ineffective form of discipline. It not only shows children that aggression is an acceptable reaction, but it teaches disrespect for others and eventually loses its effectiveness. Many people simply learn to block it out or retreat into themselves, which can cause emotional harm. Some research even shows that yelling is as harmful as corporal punishment.

Instead, allow yourself to take time or space away from the situation. You can also set your child up for success in helping guide them toward the correct decision in the first place. Give plenty of positive reinforcement, speak with calm, gentle words, and don't insult them or use swear words that will leave long-lasting memories.

Threats and Lies

If lying is a trigger for you, you are not alone. Very young children lie because they are still learning the difference between fantasy and reality, or because they are giving an imaginary version of events that they don't realize is a falsehood. Children even as young as four, though, have the capacity to lie on purpose to get out of trouble or when they know someone will be upset. They also do it if they want attention, are bragging, or if they are unhappy with something and wish for it to be different.

When your child is lying, try to understand the real reason behind the lie. Keep lines of communication open so that they don't feel fearful in coming to you. Deliver firm consequences that are accompanied by grace, forgiveness, and affection, instead of punitive measures. Don't call them a "liar," which shapes their self-concept instead of their choice. Also make sure that you aren't modeling lies yourself, even when it doesn't have to do with them. Talk about what happens when we lie, and how it can hurt others or cause more problems down the road.

Hitting and Spanking

We know this is a hot topic—there is a great deal of research to show that spanking simply doesn't do what you want it to, while also harming a great deal. Parents who chose to spank usually think that it is an effective way to discipline, and they look back on their childhoods and think, "My parents spanked me, and I turned out fine." But "fine" doesn't mean that things didn't happen on an emotional scale which we weren't aware of. Not only do the studies show harmful effects such as the reduction in the amount of gray matter in the brain and lack of impulse control associated with heightened levels of spanking (which has the opposite effect of teaching kids to "behave"), but it also shows that fewer parents are actually using this strategy each year.

Instead, actively teach them what they should do next time, teaching positive alternatives to their negative choice. Think about how else you can get the results you are looking for: connecting with your child, coming up with a plan, offering rewards instead of punishments, etc. Read the studies and learn about what the long-term consequences of spanking are. Ask yourself if you really were bonding with your parents when they spanked you or if you really felt loved. What type of relationship do you truly want with your child?

Laughing and/or Smiling at their Behavior

There are plenty of ways to help teach children good manners and etiquette while modeling what you think is appropriate and what is not. Children often act in silly or socially unacceptable ways that are cute or amusing the first couple of times but that soon become a nuisance. Again, this is a place for consistency. If we accept behaviors in some situations but not in others, our children will be confused and frustrated.

Teach them basic manners, such as 'please,' 'thank you,' 'may I...,' and 'how are you?' as well as greeting others and addressing adults with titles. (If an adult doesn't want this, they can say so, but it's a nice way to show initial manners.) Teach etiquette regarding phones, screens, and eye contact— and then model it yourself. Have conversations about being a gracious winner and a good sport when they lose, and to read body language so they can gauge others' reactions. Help them practice taking turns in conversation, and teach them what it means to treat and speak to others the way they want to be treated and spoken to, especially when they are in someone else's home.

SITUATIONS FOR CONCRETE UNDERSTANDING

In this section, you'll read an example of how a parent fuels negative behavior and then how they could have handled the situation in a more positive frame.

Not Being Consistent

Scenario 1: Patrick's parents are always telling him that his bed needs to be made each morning before he goes to school. Sometimes, mom reminds him and sends him back into his room before he leaves, sometimes either parent stands near him while he does it, and sometimes if they all forget, his mother just does it herself because she can't stand seeing such a messy bed. If she has to remind him and she's already had a hard morning, sometimes she yells, but usually not. Patrick's father ends up telling him what to do as he does it himself if Patrick is standing near him because he doesn't feel like he does a good enough job. Nothing ever happens that is serious enough to make Patrick really care about making his bed or not.

Scenario 2: Patrick's parents hold the line that his bed needs to be made each morning before he leaves for school. They believe that it is good self-discipline to have a chore that doesn't really "affect" anyone else but that leaves his space looking well-kempt and respected—plus, his mom can't stand the look of a messy bed. She hates to remind and nag, though, so when Patrick doesn't remember to do it she leaves a note on the bed she makes herself that says, "You forgot your chore and I did it for you, so please take 50 cents out of your allowance jar and you can pay me back for my time." This happened a few times before Patrick's ice cream money jar didn't have enough in it when the truck came jingling down the road. He never forgot again.

Failure to Get their Attention

Scenario 1: Nicole's parents set her up with a movie while they finished their work-from-home tasks for the day. As her father was turning the movie on, he said, "Okay, now we might not be done by the time this movie is over, so when it's finished you can color in your room, go play in the backyard, or get yourself a snack. But something healthy because it's almost dinner time. You need to turn the TV off though when the movie is over, no more shows. Got it?" Nicole stared at the television as the opening credits rolled, "Mmmhmm." Over two hours later, she was still sitting on the couch watching the sequel that began right after the first movie was over. "Nicole! We told you that you needed to turn the TV off! That's way too much screen time so soon before bed! You don't get any movie time tomorrow, do you understand?"

Scenario 2: Nicole's parents knew they would be able to complete their work-from-home tasks more quickly if she was relaxing with a movie and wouldn't interrupt them. Before they turned it on, they sat down and said, "You get to choose one movie and that's it for the evening. Which one would you like to watch?" Nicole responded with, "The Lion King." Dad said, "Okay, and how many movies did we say?" Nicole said, "One." He replied, "Yes, that's right. So, what happens when it's over?" She said, "I need to turn it off." Dad smiled and kissed her on the head. "I trust you to do that. When you've turned it off, come give me a thumbs up and you can have carrot sticks or an apple if you're hungry. Which one do you think you'll choose?" Nicole thought for a second and said, "An apple. Do you want me to bring you one, too, Dad?"

Excuses

Scenario 1: On Thursday evening, Nathan's mom came into his room and asked if he'd completed his homework for the week. He looked at his planner and said, "Yes, except for the book report and project. It's due tomorrow. Shoot. I didn't realize what day it was." Nathan's mom's eyes widened, having heard nothing about a book report. She asked him where the information was, and he pulled everything out of his backpack and handed her a crumpled note at the bottom. "Nathan, we don't even have this book! When were you supposed to do this?" Nathan shrugged, "I dunno. I think she gave it to us a couple weeks ago." Mom cried, "Why didn't you tell me? Now there's no time!" He looked at her, "I just forgot! I'm sorry. I have to turn it in though or I get a zero. Can we go to the bookstore?" His mother rolled her eyes, "No, Nathan, we can't. Here, let's just look up the Cliffs Notes." He began slowly plodding along at the computer and she scooted it over to herself, "Let me look it up, it'll go faster and it's late already." She ended up doing most of the note-taking and typing herself, with Nathan eventually just falling asleep next to her at his desk. She sighed, "Gosh, he's so irresponsible."

Scenario 2: On Thursday evening, Nathan's mom poked her head into his room, "Hi honey, is all your homework ready to turn in tomorrow?" He nodded, "Yeah, I think so." She said, "Okay, let's double check together. Grab your backpack." He slowly brought it over and began pulling out books and papers as she smoothed them out. With lowered eyes, he handed her the book report paper with tomorrow's due date in bold at the top. "Nathan! How long have you known about this?" she asked. He shrugged, "A while." She took a deep breath. "Wow, that's a bummer. There's no time now to get it done before tomorrow, that's for sure. What's your plan?" He shrugged again, "I don't know. I'll just get a zero, I guess." She nudged his shoulder. "Sorry, buddy. Not an option in this house. Try again." He looked at her, "Ask for an extension?" Mom nodded, "That could work. When will you do it?" Nathan said, "I don't know, I'm supposed to go to Brad's birthday campout this weekend." His mom sighed, "Yeah, I remembered that, too. But you know the rules, schoolwork has to be done before fun stuff. If you write a note to your teacher saying it'll be done by Monday, I'll take you to the library after school tomorrow." Nathans eyes widened, "Mom, I can't miss the campout!" Mom looked at him sadly, "I know you'll hate to miss it, but if it gets done quickly then maybe you can join them for the second evening. I know you can do it, buddy."

Yelling

Scenario 1: Adam was constantly leaving empty cartons in the fridge and pantry. This was so frustrating to his family, who would reach for something and have it be all gone, and especially when it came time to do the grocery shopping and his parents thought they had something in supply but it was actually needing to be refilled. His parents were constantly yelling at him each time it happened, "Gosh, why do you do that? That's so rude! Adam, I hate finding empty cracker boxes in the cupboard! Why are you so lazy?" Adam would just roll his eyes and walk away.

Scenario 2: Adam's parents were tired of finding empty cartons and containers all throughout the kitchen. His mom decided to be proactive about the situation, instead. The next time she went to the refrigerator and opened it and found an empty cream cheese container when she wanted to make a bagel, she called Adam into the kitchen (pulling him away from a video game he was playing). "This is empty. Empty things go in the garbage," she said calmly. "If I see it in the fridge I think we have more, but if I see it in the trash I know we're out." She handed it to him to throw away and then said, "Please add cream cheese to the grocery list." This happened a few times and Adam began feeling frustrated when he was pulled away from what he was doing to throw away a box, but after a week or so he began throwing things away on his own.

Threats and Lies

Scenario 1: Annette's mom kept finding toys all over the backyard in random places. She asked her five-year-old about it and she said that the dog was doing it, which her mother knew wasn't possible because they were in areas of their yard that their tiny dog couldn't jump or climb onto. Her mother was so frustrated and said, "Annette, I know you did this because they're your toys and the dog can't get up onto the treehouse/play structure/trampoline. Stop lying to me! Next time you lie I'm just going to throw your toys away!"

Scenario 2: Tired of finding toys left out to the elements, Annette's mother brought her outside one day. "Annette, can you tell me how these got here? Toys are supposed to get put away when you're done playing with them." Annette said, "Mom, the dog was hiding them for me to find! I couldn't find them all." Her mom smiled, "That sounds like a fun game. But you know that if you're playing with something, even with the dog or another friend, that you're still responsible for making sure they get put away. What happens if toys get left out?" Annette thought for a second, "They get wet and yucky?" Her mom nodded, "That's right. Now, do you want to put them away one at a time or get a basket to collect them all?"

Hitting and/or Spanking

Scenario 1: The Walker brothers were shouting at each other and getting rough, as they often did. They came banging into the living room, yelling, "He hit me, he punched me, I didn't do anything, he started it!" Their father was tired of hearing it, and said, "Fine, you all want to hit each other, I'll hit you, too! Line up here right now!" He proceeded to spank them all, one at a time, all in front of each other. Scenes like this were common.

Scenario 2: The Walker brothers tended to play pretty rough with each other, which was all well and good until things got out of control and a playful push or shove turned into hitting and punching and someone got hurt. Since their parents knew that intentional violence wasn't the way to teach them to stop being violent, they sat them all down one day and said, "Boys, we know you love each other, and sometimes play gets out of hand. But we don't hit people we love, even when we're angry. What can you do when you're playing and you get upset with each other?" They came up with some solutions, role played, and continued to practice. When the brothers hit, punched, or shoved each other or hurt one another, their parents encouraged them to take a deep breath, remove themselves from the situation, and then come back and hug, shake hands, or high five after an apology.

Laughing and/or Smiling at their Behavior

Scenario 1: On vacation with extended family for a week, Daniel's parents were tired and didn't want to have to deal with discipline and child-rearing, even though they were with people who they didn't see very often. They allowed Daniel a phone during dinners out at their resort, and when they were relaxing at the pool or beach Daniel was often on his phone—which was similar to his lack of limits at home. His grandparents, aunts, and uncles kept trying to talk to him but he would just respond with one-word answers and go back to his games. As the only grandchild, there weren't other kids for him to play with, but his parents just laughed nonchalantly and said that he was a regular kid who couldn't put his phone away.

Scenario 2: Although Daniel had a phone, there were firm limits around when he could use it for social media or game playing. Daniels' parents engaged him in conversation about paying attention to others when they were conversing with you, putting phones away at the table, and being present with people around you. They made sure to model this behavior themselves and stuck to putting their phones away during meal times and in the evenings when everyone was in the living room. During their family vacation, although Daniel was going to be the only kid his age present, he had plenty of practice conversing with adults and engaging with others not his age. They chose some novels and puzzle books to bring on the vacation that they said he could use when waiting for meals or relaxing by the pool, but they made a family pact to not use their phones unless it was for taking pictures.

7

EFFECTIVE PARENTING — IT STARTS WITH YOU

Although the majority of parenting books, resources, podcasts, and all-around help focus mostly on the child, the parent is actually the major player and should be treated as such. Children definitely come with personality traits, genetic markers, and other attributes that we as parents can't change no matter how hard we try, but for the most part children learn their behaviors, attitudes, and responses from us. For parents to offer the ultimate in care and guidance to their children, they must be in the right mental, physical, and psychological state. This chapter deals with how parents can ensure their overall well-being.

NEGATIVE EFFECTS OF A CHILD'S EMOTIONAL AND BEHAVIORAL PROBLEMS ON THE PARENT

Providing care for a child with serious emotional or behavioral challenges is a huge source of strain and stress for caregivers and their parents. Caregiver strain is both the inward and outward observable impact of caring for children with various disorders. Caregiver strain and stress can affect the life and functioning of a child by affecting the parent's ability to be a calm, competent, and intentional authority figure. The severity of parenting stress and/or caregiver strain might affect the quality of life for both the adult and the child(ren).

Caregiver Strain

This includes three dimensions: objective strains, subjective internalized strain, and subjective externalized strain. Objective caregiver strain deals with things such as maintaining a work-life balance or dealing with the negative effects of a child's behavior or symptoms. Subjective strain specifies the caregiver's emotions and feelings regarding caring for the child—the inner turmoil that people don't see. This is further divided into internalized and externalized strain—internalized meaning the adult's sad, worried feelings about the child and externalized referring to their own anger and/or resentment toward the child.

All the things that go along with caring for a child with high emotional needs, such as organizing appropriate childcare, making sure they are always supervised, and possibly quitting a job or changing careers to be able to organize life around what they need can take a severe strain on a person.

The more externalized, or outward, the child's symptoms (for example, oppositional defiant disorder or attention deficit hyperactivity disorder) the higher levels of predicted caregiver strain. If children had mostly internalized disorders, such as anxiety or depression, the caregiver strain was more likely to be internalized as well.

Parenting Stress

This is a set of processes that result in both negative psychological and physiological reactions that arise from trying to adapt to the demands of parenthood. Parenting stress is a common outcome when dealing with children who have both behavioral and/or emotional disorders or difficulties. Early research regarding these matters showed that high levels of parental stress were connected to high levels of child symptoms; however, newer studies also showed that the reverse was true—child symptoms predicted amounts of parental stress. Different types of symptoms, however, were correlated with different types of stress.

HOW PARENTS CAN EFFECTIVELY MANAGE THEIR EMOTIONS

Research shows us that when parents react harshly and/or with emotional intensity, children's distress tends to escalate. Thus, the problem is less likely to get resolved when both the adult and child are upset, frustrated, angry, and not communicating effectively. Parents, then, should learn key emotional management strategies so that they can help model appropriate behavior for their children. Although many parenting books, blogs, and seminars try and show parents how to teach their own children to breathe deeply, use words instead of fists, etc., probably the most effective technique is to simply manage our own emotions. Children model what they see, after all.

Some strategies to help manage your emotions are:

- **Tune in to your feelings** – Just as we have discussed teaching our children, it's important to remember that your feelings as an adult are just that—feelings. They don't (or shouldn't) have positive or negative attributes associated with them. Instead of judging your own emotions, simply identify, own, and address them; then you can respond to them appropriately. We all carry baggage and have emotional triggers, usually from our own upbringing. Deal with these on your own time so that your children aren't expected to carry their own emotional weight plus yours as well.

- **Do the unexpected** – Sometimes, the best solution is to do the opposite of what you really want to do. Every bone in your body might be screaming at you to explode, yell, throw something, slam all the doors. Instead, take a deep breath (there's a reason everyone always says to do this—it literally calms all your systems), get down on your child's level, look them in the eye and tell them you're about to give them the biggest bear hug they've ever received. If they enjoy being tickled, maybe tickle them a bit and get out some physical energy. Or tell your smart speaker to play some dance music and invite them into five minutes of "shake out" time. Sure, it sounds silly— maybe even embarrassing if you've never done it before—but I promise, the results are well worth it.

- **Give yourself a time-out, and then take a time-in with your child** – It's okay to need breaks. When you're in the trenches of infancy and toddlerhood, especially if you're the main caregiver who seems to never get a minute alone, it's perfectly okay to set your child in their crib or playpen with a kiss and a hug (even if they're still crying) and say, "Mommy/Daddy needs a break right now. It's okay if you're upset;

you're in a safe place, and I'll be right back." Put in some earplugs, drink your microwaved coffee while it's hot, or brush your teeth and put on fresh clothes in peace. Then you can come back to your child when you've reset. You can do this in later childhood, too. Simply get down on your child's level and let them know that you don't want to say or do anything mean that might hurt their feelings, so you're going to take a few minutes alone, and then you'll be back to talk to them. These strategies move you from a state of "reaction" into one that is "responsive." When you respond instead of react, you're much more likely to come up with a positive solution that guides or sets loving limits instead of punishes.

SELF-CARE STRATEGIES FOR PARENTS

Why do parents need time off and time away from their children? The reasons are plentiful! Obviously, your family needs their primary caregiver, especially if they're in the early stages of life, but you also have a responsibility—yes, responsibility—to keep yourself healthy and in a positive state of mind. No one fares well if they're a martyr who pretends that they don't have needs, too. You are a human being and you deserve rest, exercise, healthy food, adult conversation, and community.

However, the reality is that as a primary caregiver in today's society, you just cannot have it all. Sorry, not sorry. You cannot stay home with your children, keep a clean and organized home, cook from scratch, decorate for every holiday, be the PTA president, run a thriving work-from-home business, attend a weekly book club, train to run a half marathon, and get eight hours of sleep a night... as well as keep a healthy relationship with your partner and stay mentally healthy yourself. It's impossible. So, turn off the social media, decide what is truly important to you, and concentrate on the things that make *you* feel accomplished and happy. Remember that comparison is the thief of joy—your life is yours and no one else should tell you what makes it worth living. Your children were given to *you* because you are the best parent for them—no one else. So, take care of yourself and ensure that you can continue to take care of them well.

There are myriad simple and effective ways to take care of yourself—you don't have to feel overwhelmed by doing all of these on this list; just choose a few that speak to you and work them into your regular routine. You deserve it, you are worth it, and your children will thank you for making the time for yourself (possibly not out loud until they're adults and realize the benefit, but the improved dynamic and peace you feel will be thanks enough until then).

- **Practice mindfulness** – Mindfulness simply means intention. Take the tasks that you do without even thinking about it (daily hygiene, cooking, eating, cleaning the house, exercising, running errands) and begin to see them in a new light, with appreciation for the fact that *you even get to do them*! This means you're alive, you're breathing, and that you're a part of the world. This is a gift. Do each task with appreciation and grace for the small part in the bigger picture.

- **Engage your senses** – This can go along with mindfulness: a couple times a day, stop and think about one thing you see, one thing you hear, one thing you smell, one thing you are tangibly feeling, and even one thing you can taste (you'll be surprised how often you taste something even when you aren't eating!). This practice will help you to realize what brings your body joy, and then you can do more of that each day.

- **Meditate** – Meditation helps us quiet our thoughts and listen to our hearts. This can mean practicing yoga, sitting quietly and listening to calming instrumental music, drawing or coloring soothing patterns, or exercising in a beautiful place where our thoughts can settle. Whatever it is for you, it's about giving your heart and mind the opportunity to connect.

- **Spend time in nature** – We all come from nature, and getting back there can help us realize those deep lessons that often get lost in generations of "progress and "development." Nature truly does provide us with everything we need, if we are only open to Her gifts. Nature can help us realize how small we are, and how much is out of our control, which can be quite freeing.

- **Listen to music** – Music opens up something inside of us that nothing else can. It helps us process emotions, creates endorphins, and gives us a way to connect to the feelings and experiences that are common among all people. Whether it's turning on an upbeat tune and dancing away the stress, or choosing some calming instrumentals to quiet your mind, music is good for the soul.

- **Join a book club** – Stretching those muscles in your mind that don't often get stretched in the day-to-day mundane tasks of parenting and adulting can feel so refreshing! Book clubs give you a chance to learn something new, enjoy a leisurely story, and have something to look forward to each week or month. Plus, the benefit of having other adults to talk to cannot be understated!

- **Go for walks** – A little bit of exercise and some sunshine has been shown to do wonders on the mood—so much so that some doctors are even prescribing it as treatment for depression! It doesn't have to be long, even just 10 or 15 minutes around the block, but a daily walk will only do you good.

- **Write in a gratitude journal** – There's research to show that the proverbial act of "counting your blessings" will bring more blessings, or at least, it will help you realize that there are plenty of them in your life. When we choose to focus on the positives in life, we are actually training our brains to *look* for more positive things all around us. Then, when we notice (and appreciate them), it's easier for us to put more good out into the world... thus continuing the cycle.

- **Check off the to-do list** – For some people, running errands and completing tasks without children present can feel liberating! If you are someone who gets weighed down by all the daily tasks that need to happen, and your brain feels more organized and at peace when it's all completed, then it's okay to prioritize it. Just make sure that you aren't putting off other things you'd like to do for yourself in order to get the "to-dos" done. Checking off the list can also mean asking for help so that you can use your precious time for other self-care activities that are more fulfilling to you.

- **Spend a little money on yourself** – It's okay to treat yourself from time to time! Yes, budgeting, saving, and spending responsibly are all important parts of responsible adulthood. However, you work hard, and giving yourself a "yes" here and there can help make life a little more exciting.

- **Turn your bedroom into a retreat** – Your bedroom is where you go at the end of a long, trying, often exhausting day. It should be a place that welcomes you with peace, relaxation, and comfort. Install some soft lighting, add some naturally pleasing scents, and figure out some organizational solutions so that you aren't bombarded with clutter when you come into this space.

- **Savor something without apology** – When you're a parent, it often seems like nothing is sacred and everything has to be shared. Sometimes you just want to eat a piece of chocolate without hearing screaming at the same time! Allow yourself a small indulgence as a reward to look forward to at the end of the day or the end of the week, maybe in your bedroom retreat space after everyone has gone to sleep so there's no chance of interruption!

- **Detox from the screens** – We are bombarded with media, comparison, and blue light from all angles. There are many ways that technology has made life easier and better, but there are also just as many ways that it has brought stress and strife to our lives. Find time each day or each week to do a "digital detox"—leave your phone at home when you go for a walk, take social media off of your home screen, or even put a curtain over the television so it isn't in your line of sight in the living room. Most people don't ever regret the time they take away from electronics, but many regret the hours lost staring at their phones when not much is accomplished.

- **Carve out time to be alone** – So much of our lives is spent being busy, filled with caring for others, catering to their needs, or worrying about what other people think of our actions and choices. But the most important person in your life is *you*. Spending time just with yourself will help you to learn to love yourself again—there is only one of you in the whole world, and when you can get to know yourself better, you can offer your gifts to the world more freely.

- **Spend time with friends and family** – Humans are social creatures that were meant to live in community. This doesn't mean that you have to have people surrounding you at all moments of the day— solitude is important, too, as we mentioned—but friends and family are a support system that can nourish and lift you up in hard times. Let people into your life and make it a priority to develop the relationships that will be with you along this parenting journey, even if it's only a select few.

It could be helpful to make a list of all the things you spend time doing: cooking, cleaning, homework, organizing extra-curriculars, spending quality time playing with or engaging with your children, attending therapy appointments, working from home, exercising, sleeping, keeping up with friends and family, etc. Then rank these in order of impor-tance, as well as the amount of time you actually spend doing each thing. Do they match up? If not, come up with a plan that includes yourself, your partner, and your children to ensure that you are able to devote the time you want to the things that are most important. If a strict schedule doesn't feel good to you, a flexible routine is okay. Incorporate a daily or weekly calendar or checklist, even if it's just for you, and try to have a family meeting a few times a month to check in with each other and see how things are faring.

Again, modeling is the best teacher we can give our children —if they see us prioritizing our own mental, physical, and emotional health, it gives them permission to do the same. When we are raising children with emotional or behavioral struggles, this will be even more important to them developing into healthy adults.

SCENARIOS FOR CONCRETE UNDERSTANDING

Every family situation and dynamic is different. What it looks like to take care of yourself while taking care of your family—especially if you have a child or children with high behavioral and/or emotional needs is going to be unique to every situation. These scenarios should give you a jumping off point to decide what it might look like in your home.

Scenario 1: Lara's husband has begun working from home since the coronavirus pandemic. They only have one six-year-old daughter, Saoirse, but she has struggled with both ADHD and ODD since she was a few years old. Lara is also responsible for caring for her aging mother-in-law, who lives in the apartment below them. They have excellent health insurance provided by her husband's job, so although his job keeps him away upwards of 60 hours a week, and most of his salary goes to the high costs of living and caring for an elderly family member, Lara feels no guilt about using the provided 15 hours of respite care a month that their daughter's conditions qualify them for. She sets up weekly appointments with the same respite care provider each week, who is well-versed in what a child with emotional and behavioral struggles needs. Saoirse feels safe and comfortable with this "sitter" so Lara isn't worried about what will happen while she is gone. She uses the time to run on the beach, sit in a coffee shop and journal, or even volunteer at the local homeless shelter. None of these things cost money (besides an occasional hot tea or drink), and neither does the sitter. She is thankful that there is a way to get time away, so she uses it to its fullest potential to stay emotionally healthy so that she can continue to give to her family and not feel drained.

Scenario 2: Sean is a single dad whose wife, Darlene, is incarcerated. They had gotten pregnant with twins early on in their relationship before Sean realized that Darlene had an opioid addiction. She tried as hard as possible to stay clean during pregnancy, and Sean gave her all the tools and support he could. However, the twins were born with health issues that later developed into behavioral disorders and Darlene wasn't able to stay healthy or actively engaged, continually going back to using. Eventually, she was given a related prison sentence. Sean swallowed his pride and reached out to both sides of the family for help. The two families together came up with a plan to care for the twins while Sean worked, teaming up for meal prep, cleaning, and taking the boys to therapy sessions. Sean went to his own counseling sessions during these times away and found a second-hand treadmill on the community social media pages so he could run early in the mornings before work while the boys were still asleep. Things weren't ever easy, but he continued to use every resource at his disposal, including the boys' school counselors, IEPs (individualized education plans), and hand-me-down toys and games that would help develop their behavioral and life skills. Sean knew that his job wasn't to make things perfect, but to give the twins a better start than maybe he or Darlene had had. He tried to break cycles and heal his own trauma so that when the boys grew, they could concentrate on their own.

Scenario 3: Yvette originally thought that she wanted to homeschool her children, as she knew the benefits of days filled with engaged play and a more flexible approach to child-led learning. She loved the early years of staying home with her babies, and although she was often exhausted at the end of the day, she felt proud of the foundation she was able to give to her family. Money was tight on one income, but she used her coupon-cutting and meal-planning skills to help keep things in the black, as well as breastfeeding and cloth diapering the babies well into toddlerhood. As the years went on, though, and two of the five children began to show signs of needing treatment and therapies for some behavioral struggles (which both she and her husband carried in their genetic lines), she began to look for alternative schooling options that would help her children. The local public school wasn't going to offer what the children required, so she applied for need-based scholarships at some local Montessori and charter schools that specialized in attending to children with high levels of need. Yvette spent the time when her children struggling with anxiety and ADD were in school to spend quality time with the other three, and when her husband got home at the end of the day, he took the reins so that she could spend a few hours working from home as a bookkeeper. Her husband took over the dinner clean-up and bedtime routine so that he could spend time with the children while Yvette got in a quick run around the block or yoga practice to clear her mind. Again, the days were busy and filled to the brim, but as each family member got what they needed, things began to run more harmoniously.

Scenario 4: Jaleel and Sarah were your average, middle-class, dual-income couple who had three kids. One boy developed a conduct disorder during middle-elementary school, and although the other two did not have specific disorders per se, the entire family was affected by this. Jaleel and Sarah tried to keep their relationship healthy, but eventually their own conflicts and arguing made the home environment much worse. They decided to separate and work on their own individual past hurts and baggage so that they could be healthier for their children. They decided to settle custody arrangements out of court and were able to keep things civil between themselves, trading off weeks with the children. During the weeks that each parent did not have the children, they made it a priority to work ahead in their jobs, work on their respective degrees attending online school, attend their own counseling sessions, and keep physically healthy. They also went to couple's therapy and family therapy, at an office where the children could play in a safe common area when they weren't a part of the sessions.

AFTERWORD

Parenting or helping care for a child with emotional or behavioral difficulties is not for the faint of heart. It takes strength, perseverance, patience, a good handle on your own emotions and triggers, and at least a dash of a sense of humor, plus plenty of grace. However, with the right tools in your hands and in your heart, you will be able to come out on the other side feeling as if you have done your job well. Hopefully, you and your child will have a healthy, positive relationship to show for it.

Remember that every struggle has its root causes. No child is "bad" just out of nowhere. Learning the true reasons that a child is struggling might seem like opening Pandora's box, but it's the only way to get to the bottom of the issue and solve it for good. It's worth the time and effort you'll spend, even if it seems that you have to go backward at the beginning.

Parenting and caregiving don't come with instruction manuals, though, so reaching out and acquiring the resources you need and deserve is one of the best places to start. Read books (like this one), take classes, listen to podcasts, and speak with other like-minded parents to get perspective and ideas for what might work for you and your child. No two people and no two situations are the same, so listen to your intuition and above all *listen to your child*, even if that means having to read between the lines.

If, as you're learning, you realize that you have made some mistakes and there is healing to be done, acknowledge that and accept it—then move forward. It's okay to have made mistakes, to have ascribed to a certain parenting style that you thought was beneficial but was actually causing harm, or to have repeated cycles from your own childhood, only to realize now that those choices were you just doing the best you could with what you had and what you knew... back then. When you know better, you do better.

One of the best ways to raise a child who exhibits empathy and respect in their relationships with others is to model this yourself. Empathy and respect take practice—especially if you weren't raised in an environment that placed importance on these qualities. Seeing the world through the perspective of your child is an eye-opening experience—one that you probably won't be able to shut the door on once you've opened it. This is a good thing! It can sometimes seem easier to take the "because I said so" approach to most of parenting's struggles, but if we want our children to understand where we and others are coming from—and respond accordingly—then we have to do the same.

Parenting with empathy is best practiced from the beginning, from infancy. When we can hone these skills through all stages of life, they don't feel so foreign and cumbersome. However, most parents and caregivers realize that they need some help in these areas later on in their journey, so remember that it's okay to begin developing healthy emotional attachments later on in childhood. Sure, it's going to take some extra effort, but again, the rewards are more than worth it. And what's the alternative? To continue struggling, continue watching your child suffer, and to fret for years about what will become of them later in life and what will become of your parent-child dynamic? Better to accept that there is work to be done and watch the beautiful growth happen… in both of you.

Unconditional love is the best gift that any human can receive. To be fully accepted and appreciated for who we are —not what we do, how we perform, or how we measure up to everyone else in the world—what a treasure! Don't we all want to be looked at this way, deep within ourselves? We all have flaws, crosses to bear, and things that we wish were different about ourselves. This is human nature. If we want to be accepted for who we are then we need to give that to our children as well. We have brought our children into this world and are raising them with our own blood, sweat, and tears... and soon they will do the same. To love them so well that they will be able to take on their own parenting journeys (or really, just any and all of life's inevitable challenges) with strength, confidence, grace... and with parents who they can come back to for support and guidance is a picture that most people would love to carry with them.

It's not always the easiest "advice" to receive, but all of this really does start with *you*. The good news is that you've already taken the first step: reading this book! If you are spending your time learning about new ideas and filling your toolbox with resources, then it means you are a good parent already, or a caregiver who truly cares about the children whom you guide. The fact that you've opened yourself up to this journey is huge, and you should give yourself credit.

Don't keep all this to yourself, either! There are so many adults out there wanting to know what to do with their difficult child. Share this with your friends and family, leave a review on Amazon, or gift this book to someone who you know would benefit from it. The ripple effects into our world will keep going as we all keep helping each other.

You deserve a healthy, happy relationship with your child, and they deserve a parent or caregiver who finds joy in helping them grow into a competent, empathetic, respectful, positive person. You have the tools—it's simply up to you to go put them into practice. You're strong, you're capable, and you and your child are worth it.

RESOURCES

https://www.nimh.nih.gov/health/publications/disruptive-mood-dysregulation-disorder

https://www.verywellmind.com/disruptive-mood-dysregulation-disorder-4774447

https://www.hopkinsmedicine.org/health/conditions-and-diseases/oppositional-defiant-disorder

https://childmind.org/article/what-is-odd-oppositional-defiant-disorder/

https://www.healthline.com/health/conduct-disorder

https://www.aacap.org/AACAP/Families_and_Youth/Facts_for_Families/FFF-Guide/Conduct-Disorder-033.aspx#:~:text=%22Conduct%20disorder%22%20refers%20to%20a,in%20a%20socially%20acceptable%20way

https://www.nimh.nih.gov/health/topics/attention-deficit-hyperactivity-disorder-adhd/index.shtml

https://www.mayoclinic.org/diseases-conditions/adhd/symptoms-causes/syc-20350889

https://childmind.org/article/dmdd-extreme-tantrums-irritability/

https://sci-hub.se/https://doi.org/10.1016/S0962-1849(05)80124-6

https://childmind.org/article/can-help-kids-self-regulation/

https://childmind.org/article/why-do-kids-have-tantrums-and-meltdowns/

https://www.parentingscience.com/authoritarian-parenting.html

https://www.parentingforbrain.com/authoritarian-parenting-tough-love/

https://www.verywellmind.com/what-is-authoritative-parenting-2794956

https://www.parentingscience.com/authoritative-parenting-style.html

https://www.verywellfamily.com/ways-to-become-a-more-authoritative-parent-4136329

https://www.verywellmind.com/what-is-permissive-parenting-2794957#:~:text=Permissive%20parenting%20is%20a%20type,friend%20than%20a%20parental%20figure

https://www.parentingscience.com/permissive-parenting.html

https://www.healthline.com/health/parenting/uninvolved-parenting#characteristics

https://www.verywellmind.com/what-is-uninvolved-parenting-2794958#:~:text=Uninvolved%20parenting%2C%20sometimes%20referred%20to,dismissive%2C%20or%20even%20completely%20neglectful

https://www.parentingforbrain.com/uninvolved-parenting/

https://www.verywellfamily.com/types-of-parenting-styles-1095045

http://cejsh.icm.edu.pl/cejsh/element/bwmeta1.element.ojs-doi-10_15633_pch_1525/c/1525-1425.pdf

https://www.naturalchild.org/articles/guest/tamara_parnay.html

https://www.mother.ly/child/how-to-parent-with-more-empathy-grace

https://onetimethrough.com/e-empathetic-10-ways-teach-empathy/

https://www.parentingscience.com/teaching-empathy-tips.html

https://mcc.gse.harvard.edu/resources-for-families/5-tips-cultivating-empathy

https://www.ahaparenting.com/blog/When_Empathy_Doesnt_Work

https://www.uaex.edu/life-skills-wellness/personal-family-well-being/docs/The%20Emotional%20Ties%20between%20Parents%20and%20Children.pdf

https://psychology.jrank.org/pages/472/Parent-Child-Relationships.html

https://athealth.com/topics/different-types-of-parent-child-relationships-3/

https://www.momjunction.com/articles/helpful-tips-to-strengthen-parent-child-bonding_0079667/

https://www.psychologytoday.com/us/blog/peaceful-parents-happy-kids/201706/10-habits-strengthen-parent-child-relationship

https://www.verywellfamily.com/tips-to-strengthen-families-617242

https://www.askdrsears.com/topics/parenting/attachment-parenting/attachment-parenting-babies/

https://evolutionaryparenting.com/how-to-love-your-child-unconditionally/

https://onetimethrough.com/loving-kids-unconditionally/

https://www.parents.com/parenting/better-parenting/simple-ways-to-show-your-child-your-love/

https://www.psychologytoday.com/us/blog/peaceful-parents-happy-kids/201403/5-secrets-love-your-child-unconditionally

https://afineparent.com/close-knit-family/how-to-love-unconditionally.html

https://www.verywellfamily.com/why-does-consistency-matter-in-parenting-4135227

https://www.verywellfamily.com/why-your-child-is-not-listening-to-you-620116

https://www.verywellfamily.com/prevent-child-making-excuses-1094981

https://www.verywellfamily.com/how-to-discipline-without-yelling-at-kids-620125

https://www.verywellfamily.com/what-to-do-when-kids-lie-620107

https://www.verywellfamily.com/why-parents-spank-reasons-for-corporal-punishment-620129

https://www.verywellfamily.com/teaching-children-manners-620111

https://www.verywellfamily.com/how-parents-encourage-bad-behavior-in-kids-620123

https://www.empoweringparents.com/article/learn-to-love-your-difficult-childthe-difference-between-love-and-acceptance/

https://www.5lovelanguages.com

https://www.ncbi.nlm.nih.gov/pmc/articles/PMC3975620/

https://www.zerotothree.org/resources/521-managing-your-own-emotions-the-key-to-positive-effective-parenting

https://www.healthychildren.org/English/family-life/family-dynamics/Pages/Importance-of-Self-Care.aspx

https://www.verywellfamily.com/self-care-for-parents-4178010

https://www.mghclaycenter.org/parenting-concerns/10-self-care-tips-for-parents/

https://www.ncbi.nlm.nih.gov/pmc/articles/PMC5658126/

https://www.goodtherapy.org/learn-about-therapy/issues/disruptive-mood-dysregulation

https://www.autism360.com/oppositional-defiant-disorder-treatment-and-odd-case-study/#Meet_Arthur_8211_A_Child_with_ODD

https://corecapacities.com/wp-content/uploads/04%
20Oppositional%20Defiant%20Disorder%20-%20M.,%
20Age%203%20-%20Soriano,%20M.pdf

https://files.eric.ed.gov/fulltext/EJ844406.pdf

https://journalofethics.ama-assn.org/article/coping-childs-
conduct-disorder/2006-10

https://www.psychiatry.org/patients-families/adhd/patient-
story

https://www.cdc.gov/violenceprevention/aces/index.html

https://www.firstthingsfirst.org/early-childhood-matters/
brain-development/

Made in the USA
Las Vegas, NV
19 August 2022